JAPJI

The Path of Devotional Meditation

JAPJI

The Path of Devotional Meditation

Surinder Deol
Daler Deol

Mount Meru Books
Washington, D. C.

Mount Meru Books
P. O. Box 27502
Washington, D. C. 20038-7502

FIRST EDITION

ISBN 0-9661027-0-3

Library of Congress Catalog Card Number 97-92703

Cover and book design by
George Parakamannil

Printed in the United States of America

For Seekers
of the
Enlightenment Spirit

Contents

Acknowledgments   9

Introduction   11

Part One

Japji: Meditations   27

Part Two

Japji: Explanatory Notes on Meditations   59

Mool Mantra Meditation   135

Thirty-nine Most Beautiful Names   137

Part Three

Japji: A Guide to Spiritual Living   139

Summing-Up   165

Bibliography   167

Acknowledgments

We would like to express our deep gratitude to our parents who prepared us to search for the real meaning of human relationships and our relationship with God. They gave us the courage and temperament to ask some basic, yet perplexing, questions about life's purpose and what it means to be born into a faith that one didn't choose. Our parents had an abiding interest in spirituality that gave us, at an early age, an experience of the subtle and the mystical. Early impressions lingered on to become a passion for discovering and sharing spiritual knowledge later in our life.

We are very proud of having raised two wonderful kids. They have taught us many things over the years. Raj, our son, with his engineering and business management background, has taught us the importance of applying rational and analytical approaches to solving life's problems. Rinku, our daughter, with her artistic and caring self, has made us aware of the transformative power of love. Shuchi, Raj's life partner, who is deeply committed to pediatrics as a profession, has shared with us her experiences of seeing the smile on the face of a child as the fulfillment of a devotional act. We would like to say thanks to them as they make us feel bigger than ourselves, for all their loving and caring.

Surinder is grateful to his friends at the Spiritual Unfoldment Society (SUS) for their encouragement. For several years now, SUS has provided him with an exciting forum to debate ideas and experiences at the intersection of soul, spirituality, and the path to enlightenment. His conversations with Richard Barrett, SUS founder, on "liberating the soul" reinforced his desire to examine various enlightenment traditions, with a focus on their similarities and differences.

Daler would like to thank her friends at Chetana, a voluntary non-profit organization in Washington Metropolitan Area, for their active participation in several cultural and spiritual activities that resulted in better understanding of the challenges of living and working in a multicultural society.

Introduction

In many spiritual traditions, sunrise is a sacred moment. It is the time of the day when nature wakes up from its nightly slumber. Birds sing and the journey of life begins for another day. At a mythical level, there is a death and a rebirth. The night that dies becomes a part of our collective memory. The day that is born brings hope and joy. We are awakened to the mystery of life, our consciousness slowly spreads its wings, and we begin to savor the taste of life. What better time could we find to seek oneness with our Creator, whose love and care makes it possible for us to add yet another day to our lives!

> When dawn breaks,
> we sing glories of Your greatness.
>
> Japji
> *Meditation 4*

As a morning prayer, *Japji* (from the word *"jap,"* meaning chanting, reciting, or meditating) is unique in many ways. This composition represents the very essence of Guru Nanak's spiritual and cosmological beliefs. It is the foundation of Sikh (literally meaning "a disciple") faith. Consisting of a prologue, 38 meditations, and an epilogue, *Japji* commends the path of unconditional love—a complete submission to the command of a loving God. It is the opening composition in the *Adi Granth*, meaning the "first scripture." The *Granth* contains mystical

11

compositions of Sikh gurus and other revered saints, such as Kabir. It was compiled by the fifth guru, Guru Arjun Dev, and was later vested with the power and sanctity of a living guru and transformed into *Guru Granth Sahib* by the tenth and last guru, Guru Gobind Singh, in 1708. The reverence shown to the *Granth* as a living embodiment of Supreme Guru is unmatched by any other world scripture.

Devotional Meditation

Contemplate solely the name of God—
Fruitless are all other rituals.

Raga Suhi

The path preached by Guru Nanak is one of total devotion in which recitation of the Name is considered a form of meditation. According to a survey presented by Daniel Goleman in his book *The Meditative Mind: The Varieties of Meditative Experience*, the roots of devotional paths can be traced to ancient classics such as *Srimad Bhagavatam*, that recommended chanting the name of Krishna. Recitation of the Name is also advocated in many other spiritual traditions. The Koran contains the Ninety-nine Most Beautiful Names of Allah. Sufis use these names in what they call "remembrance"—a time of intense meditation. Christians offer prayers in the name of Jesus Christ, remembering him as a Son of God. Buddhists make use of mantras such as Om Ah Hum Vajra Guru Padma Siddhi Hum (The embodiment of the body, speech, and mind of the Buddhas, O Padmasambhava, please grant all blessings!).

Devotional meditation originates in the heart and soul of a devotee, and it is directed outward to a Higher Being (the flow of feeling and emotions is from the subjective to the objective). For the performer, it is what transpersonal psychologists call a "peak experience," in which one is elevated from the immediate surroundings and transported to a world of soul consciousness.

Westerners often ask: How can reciting a name, chanting a *mantra*, singing a *shabad*, or participating in a *kirtan* make any difference? It is a valid question. There are three answers.

First, recitation of a sacred word such as Om, Jesus, Allah, *Ikk Oankar*, concentrates our mind as nothing else and narrowly focuses our attention on the object of this recitation. For example, if we say "Waheguru" (the most popular description of God among Sikhs, which means "Greetings to the Greatest Guru of All Beings"), we direct our gratitude and salutation to a single source of cosmic energy that is very difficult to visualize in the normal course. The picture that emerges in our mind is not the picture of an individual being but of the whole cosmic sphere. Once we hear the Name, we have an opportunity to engage in some creative imagery of our own. We can elevate ourselves mentally and float like a cloud. We can try to picture in our mind how the Supreme Being might look. We can see the "sound and light show" of the universe in perpetual motion, while reflecting on the unbreakable bond between the Creator and the creation.

Second, recitation of the Name bridges the gulf between the individual and the Deity. It can turn easily into a creative dialogue or conversation, whereby the Deity speaks to the individual and provides answers to very difficult questions. For a person of deep faith, it is the voice of the inner self. But in order to listen to this voice, whether it comes from inside or outside, we have to be in touch with our divine self. What better way to do this than to call the Supreme Beloved by the given Name?

Third, recitation of the Name is also a form of meditation and, thus, it has all the benefits associated with meditation. But it needs to be said that Guru Nanak does not recommend deep and socially isolating meditative practices that are common in Hinduism and Buddhism. The best meditation is recitation of the Name in the quiet of one's home or in the company of other believers. Guru Nanak's spirituality is deeply rooted in the family and the community. Therefore, the practitioner is empowered to have a "peak" experience as well as a "plateau" experience (sharing one's spiritual pursuits with one's family, friends, and community).

Guru Nanak's Life and Work

An understanding of the mystical significance of *Japji* requires a brief introduction to Guru Nanak's life and the central core of his teachings. He was born on April 15, 1469, in a village near Lahore, now in Pakistan. The place was later renamed Nankana Sahib in the Guru's memory. Most accounts of the Guru's life are based on contemporary hagiographical sketches *(janam sakhis)*, written for pedagogical purposes. As a precocious child, Nanak uttered words of wisdom that were beyond the reckoning of people around him. The family priest, who read the horoscope, predicted:

> Both Hindus and Muslims will revere him. His name will be known on earth and in heaven. As he walks, the ocean will part to give him the way. So will the earth and sky. He will worship and acknowledge only the Supreme Being, and he will command others to do the same.

Nanak surprised his teachers with his sharp and philosophic mind. Married at the age of sixteen, he had two sons. It soon became clear that young Nanak did not have much interest in the material reality of a householder's life. His sister invited him to come to Sultanpur and persuaded her husband to get Nanak a job with the local nawab. Although the job involved only mundane accounting, Nanak spent most of his time carrying on his search for the True One.

In August 1507, Nanak had a mystical experience involving a revelation while he bathed in the Bein river. After three days, Nanak emerged from under the river as a messiah, chanting "There is neither Hindu nor Muslim," to the great surprise of his acquaintances who had given him up as drowned. After this great transformational event of self-enlightenment, he was always addressed as Guru Nanak. The Guru set out on a long journey of discovery, which took him to several places of Hindu pilgrimages within India and presumably also to the Muslim sacred cities of Mecca and Medina.

It is difficult to account for the major influences on the Guru's life, but he shared many of his beliefs with those in mystical and devotional traditions that also produced saints like Kabir. There is no evidence to corroborate guesses regarding the Guru's meeting with Kabir, although there is some possibility that they were contemporaries. The Guru witnessed the brutal tyranny of Mughal Emperor Babar's invasion of India, and he wrote about it. The last part of the Guru's life was spent in Kartarpur, where he laid the institutional foundation of the Sikh faith. *Japji* was written during this period. The Guru joined his Supreme Beloved on September 22, 1539. The following account of this event appears in Puratan text:

> Guru Nanak went and sat under a withered acacia, which immediately produced leaves and flowers, becoming verdant again. Guru Angad (his principal disciple and the successor) prostrated himself. The assembled congregation sang hymns of praise and Guru Nanak passed into an ecstatic trance. While thus transported, he sang the hymn entitled "The Twelve Months." It was early morning and the time had come for his departure. Hindus and Muslims, who had put their faith in the Divine Name, began to debate what should be done with the Guru's body. "We shall bury him," said the Muslims. "No, let us cremate his body," said the Hindus. "Place flowers on both sides of my body," said Guru Nanak, "flowers from the Hindus on the right side and flowers from the Muslims on the left. If tomorrow the Hindus' flowers are still fresh let my body be burned, and if the Muslims' flowers are

still fresh let it be buried." Guru Nanak then covered himself with a sheet and passed away. Those who had gathered around him prostrated themselves, and when the sheet was removed they found that there was nothing under it. The flowers on both sides remained fresh, and both Hindus and Muslims took their respective shares. (Adapted from McLeod 1984, p. 25)

Guru Nanak was succeeded by nine other gurus before the tenth and last guru, Guru Gobind Singh decided to end the line of succession in 1699. He invested all religious and social authority in *Guru Granth Sahib*, the supreme testament of Sikh theology.

The Nature of God

According to Guru Nanak, God is formless and unfathomable, yet gracious and loving. God, as the ultimate preceptor, speaks through saints from time to time; Guru Nanak was one of those saints, and his lyrical speech enables us to know the unknowable, based on his own spiritual experiences. Recitation of the sacred Name, which is the quintessential experience of reading or listening to God's word, removes the need for all other actions.

For saints in the devotional tradition, a tradition marked by selfless love, God exists either without attributes or with attributes, that is, in human form. Guru Nanak's conception of God is unambiguous. A belief in one God is the first principle of his devotion, but it is also a devotion for a God that is formless, immortal, beyond the cycle of life and death, self-illumined, and true. This view is strongly attributeless; therefore, it should not be confused with the worship of a personal god. The Guru's emphasis on listening to recitation of the Name acknowledges that God's unseen presence can be experienced at a very personal level. Although God is not manifest, there is a divine presence in our daily life. The most important manifestation of God is through the medium of the holy word that is revealed to a preceptor, who then shares it with the rest of humanity.

The Five Stages of Spiritual Journey

All human beings, with some initial preparation, are capable of undertaking the spiritual journey. In Meditations 34 through 37, Guru Nanak describes five separate and distinctive stages of our spiritual journey:

> The first realm is that of moral living and rightful action *(dharam khand)*. It is the playing field for the principles of conventional morality. If we abide by the accepted religious and moral principles, common to all religions, and are able to differentiate between good and evil, we may find ourselves at the start of a journey that eventually takes us closer to God.

> The second realm is that of divine knowledge *(jnan khand)*. In this realm, one relentlessly searches for the mystical and spiritual knowledge. The true knowledge pertains to the nature of God, origin of the universe, cosmic laws, the purpose of human life, and the central role of the Creator in keeping this vast creation in balance. Once we enter this realm, the mysteries of creation are revealed to us.

> The third realm is that of the spiritual beauty, effort, and unfoldment *(saram khand)* in which one develops the spiritual strength to see beyond the material reality and gain spiritual expansion. The spirit is steeped in unparalleled aesthetic experiences. Beauty is generally considered to be an attribute of the human body. But the beauty of the spirit or soul is an unfoldment in a different dimension. It is sheer radiance produced by the human spirit when it is embraced by an ocean of divine light. In this realm, the spirit truly transforms itself and gets ready to realize its potential.

> The fourth realm is that of divine grace *(karam khand)*. An endless flow of higher energy is opened for the chosen few who reach this point. Not everyone is worthy of divine grace. Grace is the sovereign prerogative of the Supreme. We can pray

for it but can't demand it. Grace is a gift, a reward, but not a personal accomplishment.

The fifth and the last realm is that of eternal truth *(sach khand)*, which is the center of God's formless state and of the whole creation. In this realm, there are infinite places of heavenly beauty wherein reside fully realized beings who have successfully made the transition from the lower to the upper realms. This is the stage of total self-realization and unity consciousness.

Creation Mythology

The Guru's creation mythology complements his conception of the formless God. He suggests an identifiable moment of creation, when a tremendous burst of energy started the evolutionary process. This process involved the unique role of the Creator; the creation is the most magnificent work of God. The Creator made the world out of many elements, infusing divine light into every particle, including the human being. Humans, therefore, did not evolve from lower species. Only human beings are blessed to pursue the divine path because of their potential for divine consciousness, given to them at the time of creation. It is this potential in all of us, the infusion of divine energy at the start of the creation, that enables us to seek God. We can experience this excitement of creation when we are deeply in tune with our soul. What happened billions of years ago in a physical dimension happens every day in our spiritual quest.

Creation and evolution go together. Creation is about dynamic particles that provide a concrete shape to reality. Evolution, as the Creator's work in progress, is an expression of the divine will. It is also the spiritual highway that makes the journey of the soul to higher planes possible. As we come closer to our Supreme Beloved through successive stages of physical and spiritual evolution, the secrets of creation are slowly revealed to us. The Creator never stops creating. What is accomplished at the physical level is also replicated at the soul level.

Guru Nanak and Hinduism

Guru Nanak was born into and lived in a social and cultural environment that was predominantly Hindu in its beliefs and practices. Hinduism, a Persian word meaning "what Indians do," is a complex set of beliefs, doctrines, and practices. It is a mixture of religion, philosophy and culture. All Sikhs are followers of Guru Nanak, but the Guru has a sizable following outside the Sikh community as well. Many Hindus worship Guru Nanak as an incarnate saint.

We need note three principal differences: First, Guru Nanak preaches a strictly monotheistic faith, whereas Hinduism, in theory, is monotheistic in the sense that there is a unified concept of God, Brahman, or the Ultimate Reality. In practice, however, Hindus worship several gods and goddesses, treating them more or less as autonomous beings. Second, Guru Nanak makes spirituality a family-centered pursuit that encourages people to lead a spiritual life while fulfilling their communal and societal obligations. In Guru Nanak's theology, there is no concept of *sanyas* (giving up the domestic life); enlightenment needs to be pursued while being a model householder. Third, Guru Nanak firmly believes in the equality of all human beings who are capable of attaining *moksha*, or spiritual liberation. As a consequence, he rejects both the caste system and the priestly power that sustains the caste system.

There are many areas of agreement between traditional Hindu faith and the path preached by Guru Nanak. For one thing, Hindus believe in three distinct paths of liberation, namely, the path of knowledge *(jnan yoga)*, the path of devotion *(bhakti yoga)*, and the path of action *(karma yoga)*. Guru Nanak regards these three paths as legitimate ways of attain-

19

ing spiritual enlightenment, but considers the path of devotion, coupled with moral living, as more potent and practical. Guru Nanak's hymns are highly devotional in content; he also emphasizes the need for leading a virtuous life.

In an another area of agreement, Guru Nanak accepts the doctrine of *karma*, which says that we are rewarded or punished in the future life based on the quality of our actions in this life. Liberation *(moksha)* means cessation of the cycle of life and death. There is agreement, also, in that Guru Nanak's faith and Hinduism share many aspects of social, cultural, and religious life. For instance, Guru Nanak's followers show reverence to Hindu gods and goddesses and accept them as manifestations of the One Supreme Being, elaborately described by Guru Nanak in his work. Many Hindu and Sikh festivals are common (*Diwali*, the festival of lights, is celebrated by both religions, although for somewhat different reasons). Sikhs have the same aversion to eating beef as Hindus. In fact, vegetarianism is a requirement in both religions, although it is unevenly practiced. Marriages between Hindu and Sikh families are commonplace.

Fourth, Guru Nanak and Hinduism subscribe to identical creation myths. For Guru Nanak, this universe is the creation of God; for Hindus, this is the work of the Divine, manifested as god Brahma. Fifth, Guru Nanak shares with traditional Hinduism the four goals of life: righteousness *(dharma)*, economic success *(artha)*, pleasure within the confines of a married life *(kama)*, and spiritual enlightenment *(moksha)*. There is, however, great emphasis by Guru Nanak on the importance of divine grace as a prerequisite for liberation.

Guru Nanak's vision of human beings is strongly egalitarian. All human beings, irrespective of caste, color, creed, or gender, must be treated equally as moral beings, transcending these distinctions. The Hindu society of his time was divided into different castes. Only the highest class *(brahmins)* was qualified to read the scriptures. People from the lowest class were not entitled to hear the word of God. Women in general were treated as inferior, with no capacity for independent spiritual pursuits. On the role of women in religion and society, Guru Nanak said:

> From woman is man born, inside her is he conceived;
> to woman is man engaged, and woman he marries.
> Woman is man's companionship.
> From woman originates new generations.
> Should woman die, another is sought;
> by woman's help is man kept in restraint.
> Why revile her of whom are born great ones of the earth?
> From woman is born woman, no human being without woman is born.
>
> *Raga Asa*

Although several Hindu scriptures (including the Vedas) did not sanction caste systems based on heredity, the social structure of four classes had solidified to such an extent that heredity had become civil society's sole organizing principle. The Guru broke this hierarchy of the caste system and conceptualized only one class of humans, who lived under the care and protection of one loving God.

According to Guru Nanak, no man or woman is a fallen being. We are all capable of leading a virtuous life. The Guru's conception of a virtuous life consists of human beings resisting the five dreadful streams of fire, which are propensities or springs of action, namely lust, greed, attachment, anger, and pride. These forces become dominant when our mind is not under our control. These evils are overcome by recitation of the Name; as fire is put out by water, so the Name frees us from these limiting propensities.

The Guru considered the established priestly order as highly corrupt and morally decadent. Priests did not practice what they preached. They did not understand the meaning of scriptures that they mechanically used for their own purposes. They encouraged perpetuation of practices and rituals that did not bear any spiritual fruit. The Guru exposed the hollowness of some of these rituals. Instead of doing any good, they were harmful to people's spiritual growth because they took them away from God.

According to Guru Nanak, holy life can be pursued in the course of our normal life—being a householder, earning a rightful living, and meeting the challenges of daily life. This was another departure from the Hindu way of life in which human life was divided into four episodes, such as *brahmcharya* (the student life), *grihastha* (the family life), *vanaprastha* (retirement from the working life), and *sanyas* (a life free from all worldly attachments). Guru Nanak advocates leading an exemplary life based on good education; a married life, built around love and mutual respect; moral and ethical upbringing of children; and a retired life of active community service, prayer, and meditation.

Guru Nanak and Buddhism

Although it is uncommon to find parallels between Guru Nanak and Gautama Buddha, there are many similarities. Both Gautama Buddha and Guru Nanak preached new paths that challenged the established order; both challenged all forms of ritualism; both spoke to ordinary people in a language that they understood; both warned their disciples against blind following of tradition; both advocated the importance of rightful livelihood; both preached equality between men and between men and women; both advocated the middle road, a path that avoids extremes of asceticism and indulgence; and both spoke about a life of infinite compassion and enlightenment that comes from within oneself.

The basic teaching of Buddhism is found in the Four Noble Truths: this life is characterized by suffering; suffering is caused by craving, desire, and attachment; suffering can cease because its cause can cease; and the path of truth that leads to cessation of suffering is the Eightfold Path—right understanding, right thought (these two conditions lead to wisdom), right speech, right action, right livelihood (these three conditions constitute morality), right effort, right mindfulness, and right concentration (the last three conditions lead to concentration, or *samadhi*).

In Guru Nanak's hymns, there is repeated emphasis on many of the same things included in the Eightfold Path, but the Guru takes a much more optimistic view of life than Gautama Buddha. First, according to Guru Nanak, life is made up of suffering as well as happiness and bliss, depending on the choices made by us. This life is an opportunity to show our devotion to our Creator and to pray for divine blessings. This life is also the start of our spiritual journey. Second, Guru Nanak commends the path of devotion, with remembrance of the Name as its central discipline, and not the path of intense meditation recommended by Buddhism. Third, in the Eightfold Path, there is no appeal to divine grace, which is an essential prerequisite for completing the spiritual journey described by Guru Nanak. Fourth, unlike Guru Nanak, Buddhism has no concept of God as a Supreme Being. Most Buddhist deities are spirits that are conditioned by their actions and as such are not yet fully liberated.

In spite of these differences, there is much common ground between Guru Nanak and Buddhism, not only with regard to spiritual beliefs but also social organization. Guru

Nanak's conception of *sangat* (a congregation of like-minded souls) is not very different from Buddhist *sangha* (a religious community), where the Buddhist way of life is practiced.

Guru Nanak and Islam

Guru Nanak was a Sufi, in the sense that he was deeply in love with his Creator, and his hymns have the same mystical quality found in the inspired poetry of Sufi saints. He celebrates the beauty and grandeur of the Supreme Beloved in the tradition of Sufi saints, such as Attar and Rumi. In addition, the hymns of Muslim Sufi saints, such as Sheikh Farid, were included in the *Granth* along with the hymns of Sikh gurus and Hindu saints. In one of his compositions, Guru Nanak debated the question of who is a true Muslim. He wrote:

> Make the mosque of compassion your prayer mat;
> make honest living your motto, as the Koran says.
> Let modesty be your circumcision,
> and noble path your Ramadan fast—
> such a Muslim you ought to be!
> Let good work be your Kaaba, and truth your prophet;
> let good actions be your affirmation and prayer;
> let your rosary please God.
> Only then, says Nanak, your honor before God be
> vindicated.
>
> *Raga Majh*

Guru Nanak respected the inner core of Islam as a true religion, based on divine revelation to the Prophet. Many Muslim saints showed respect to Guru Nanak during his life, as a truly enlightened soul.

There is a viewpoint that Guru Nanak created a synthesis of the best in Hinduism and Islam. There is no concrete evidence to support this thesis. If anything, Sikhism owes its origin to the spiritual enlightenment of its founder, who wanted to transcend the traditional institutionalized differences among people based solely on their religion. "There is no Hindu, there is no Muslim," said Guru Nanak. We are all children of one God, who is our sole provider and protector, and we owe our unqualified allegiance to that one Supreme Deity.

How to Use This Book

This book is aimed at facilitating our readers' search for a path to enlightenment, using the spiritual insights offered by Guru Nanak. These insights have helped numerous devotees attain soul consciousness over the past five hundred years. We have tried to simplify the Guru's message for a contemporary Western audience, particularly people with minimal familiarity with Eastern spirituality. Spiritual ideas, whether of the East or West, are a common heritage of all humanity. This book is not about converting you to a new faith; it's about showing you a nonsectarian path that you might consider taking.

We are aware that readers will use this book in different ways. However, as a road map, we suggest the following sequence:

Read Part One (*Japji* meditations) once or twice to familiarize yourself with the main ideas. This is recommended both for the uninitiated and for those who are familiar with Guru Nanak's spirituality. You can tape the text in your own voice and listen to the tape in the morning while driving or commuting to work. You will be surprised to see what a positive difference listening to the Name will bring to your daily life.

Go to Part Two and select one meditation for understanding and experiencing every day. Read the meditation and the commentary.

Part Three contains some key ideas drawn from Guru Nanak's spirituality and other wisdom traditions for application

25

in daily life. For instance, leading a virtuous life, becoming socially responsive and a catalyst for positive social change, and making nature our spiritual guide and companion.

This is the first interpretation of *Japji* that is aimed primarily at the North American reader. We have tried to balance the challenge of following a spiritual path while leading a material and competitive life in an advanced industrial society with all its distractions. Also, this interpretation of *Japji* is gender-neutral. Guru Nanak believed in a formless God, a conception that truly transcended distinctions of any kind, and we have respected this basic tenet in our writing.

Japji is not an easy text to render in another language. The beauty and depth of meaning is hard to retain in translation while trying to save the tonal quality of the original text. We have tried to match the depth of meaning and aural experience of the original. No such attempt is likely to yield perfect results. And this one does not. But if our effort has come anywhere near fulfilling readers' expectations, we will have reason to feel satisfied. In addition, if as a result of this book, readers come to understand and appreciate the core spiritual teachings of Guru Nanak, we will have reason to be especially pleased. Understanding a religious tradition is like building a bridge that narrows the distances and brings people together— something that is badly needed in this meaninglessly violent world of today.

Surinder & Daler Deol
August 15, 1997   *Potomac, Maryland*

Part One

Japji

Meditations

Japji
Meditations

Prologue

In the name of the One True Supreme Being,
who is the Creator of all other beings,
without fear and hatred;
of timeless form,
unborn, self-existent;
attainable
only through divine grace!

Meditation 1

Meditate.

You were True
at the beginning
and in the primal age.
Says Nanak of the Supreme,
You are True
and You will ever remain True!

We cannot gain understanding
through monotonous contemplation.
True silence is not attained
through trance-like meditation.

Neither through worldly possessions
is our hunger appeased,
nor through a million other mental feats
is enlightenment achieved.

How to prove our truth before You
and lift the veil of darkness?
Only submission to the divine order,
O Nanak, can give us awareness!

Meditation 2

Divine order that creates life
is not easy to name.
Divine order that gives life
confers honor and fame.

Divine order makes us high or low,
happy or sad again.
Divine grace saves some,
others live and are born again.

Divine order encompasses
and rules us all.
O Nanak, believers have
no ego-mind at all!

Meditation 3

Those who have the depth of understanding,
they sing of Your grace and benefaction.
Those who know Your noble attributes,
they sing of Your knowledge and deep absorption.

Those who know of Your ability to create and destroy,
they sing of Your gift of renewal and regeneration.

While some sing of Your detachment and distance,
others sing of Your omnipresence and attention.

There is no end to our praise and our description;
millions have sung Your praises with veneration.
You give to us untiringly, but the recipients get wearied;
through the ages, we have lived on Your benediction.

The movement of this universe is divinely willed.
O Nanak, there is self-realization and perfection!

Meditation 4

The True One's name is repeated
with boundless affection.
Those who ask for gifts,
receive endless benediction.

What can we offer
for a glimpse of the court divine?
What prayer can we offer
to receive Your love pristine?

When dawn breaks,
we sing glories of Your greatness.
Although karma influences,
liberation is attained with divine graciousness.

O Nanak, be it known:
the True One is the fountain of truthfulness!

Meditation 5

Neither installed nor crafted by skill,
You are immaculate and self-existent.

Those who serve You are truly meritorious.
O Nanak, sing praises of the magnificent!

Sing and hear the glories of the One
who takes away misery and gives fulfillment.
The sound of the sacred word is divine knowledge,
and the word itself is all-pervasive and resplendent.

God is Shiva, Vishnu, and Brahma;
Goddess is Parvati, Lakshmi, and Sarasvati.

Even if I understand the True One,
how do I describe Thee?

The Guru gave me one advice:
there is one God of all creation,
let me not forget.

Meditation 6

Holy bathing is fruitless
if Your pleasure is not obtained.
Divine creation that I behold
is not without destiny attained.

With Your guidance,
the hidden mental treasure is regained.

My Guru gave me one advice:
there is one God of all creation,
let me not forget.

Meditation 7

Even if our life span
covers four ages times ten.

Even if we gain
nine continents, with all souls beholden.

Even if our good name and deeds
have won us worldly recognition.
Without Your blessing and grace,
all this adds up to pure indiscretion.

We will be the lowest of all beings
and notoriously infamous.
O Nanak, the unmerited can gain true merit
and become truly virtuous!

But is there any one
who can bestow any virtue on You?

Meditation 8

Hearing Your name
makes one a spiritually realized being and a yogi.
Hearing Your name
reveals this earth, a mythical bull, and the sky.

Hearing Your name,
we know hidden worlds and regions.
Hearing Your name,
we conquer death's legions.

O Nanak, devotees ever are
in a blissful state!
Hearing Your name,
our sorrows and sins negate.

Meditation 9

Hearing Your name,
we are like Shiva, Brahma, and Indra transformed.

Hearing Your name,
even lower beings are divinely ordained.

Hearing Your name,
we understand the body's secrets.
Hearing Your name,
we acquire spiritual secrets.

O Nanak, devotees ever are
in a blissful state!
Hearing Your name,
our sorrows and sins negate.

Meditation 10

Hearing Your name, we gain truth,
contentment, and discernment.
Hearing Your name equals bathing
at sixty-eight places of sacrament.

Hearing Your name
brings veneration and admiration.
Hearing Your name,
we attain poised meditation.

O Nanak, devotees ever are
in a blissful state!
Hearing Your name,
our sorrows and sins negate.

Meditation 11

Hearing Your name makes one open
a spiritually enriching theme.

Hearing Your name makes one illuminated,
Spiritual Guide and Supreme.

Hearing Your name makes the spiritually blind
find their worldly way.
Hearing Your name, fathomless deep truths
come under our sway.

O Nanak, devotees ever are
in a blissful state!
Hearing Your name,
our sorrows and sins negate.

Meditation 12

A believer's bliss
is hard to relate.
All our efforts
will surely negate.

There is no paper,
pen, or penmanship
to describe the believer's bliss
and worship.

Such is the power
of Your immaculate denomination,
that we know it
only through total submission.

Meditation 13

A believer gains wisdom,
consciousness, and awareness.
A believer gains inner
and outer mindfulness.

A believer does not go
stumbling and hobbling.
A believer is not terrorized
by death's calling.

Such is the power
of Your immaculate denomination,
that we know it
only through total submission.

Meditation 14

A believer's path is unfettered
and self-directing.
A believer departs this world
with honor and lauding.

A believer does not stray
into ritualistic ceremonies.
A believer follows
the virtuous testimonies.

Such is the power
of Your immaculate denomination,
that we know it
only through total submission.

Meditation 15

A believer reaches the gates
of enlightenment and immortality.
A believer liberates loved ones
from life-death brutality.

A believer liberates self
and disciples seeking divine solace.

A believer, O Nanak, does not have
to wander for divine grace!

Such is the power
of Your immaculate denomination,
that we know it
only through total submission.

Meditation 16

They are blessed
whom You select.
They are honored
in Your court for their intellect.

They brighten the heavenly court
with their spiritual flame.
They find their minds dipped
in the meditation of Your name.

They try to describe You
after a good deal of reflection.
But Your doings are beyond
human enumeration.

Dharma's bull
is born of compassion,
and it holds the earth
in equalization.

This discovery enlightens
and makes us truthful.
How much load is carried
by the mythical bull?

But there are planets
and galaxies afar.

Who have carried
their loads so far?

There are different species
and colors they enshrine,
written by the ever-flowing pen
of the Divine.

Does anyone know how complete
the full account might be?
If an account is written,
how extensive might that be?

How powerful is the measure
of Your manifestation?
Who can estimate the greatness
of Your benediction?

You created the universe
with a single injunction,
and there emerged many a flowing river
and inundation.

What power do I have to describe You
and Your creation?

My powerlessness precludes
even a simple act of sacrifice!

Whatever pleases You
will public good secure.
Glory of the Formless One
shall forever endure.

Meditation 17

Countless are meditations
and countless are ways of devotion.

Countless are worships
and countless are ways of renunciation.

Countless are scriptures
and countless those who are spiritual seekers.
Countless are yogis
who are indifferent to worldly encounters.

Countless are devotees
who ponder on things veritable.
Countless are the pious
and countless are those who are charitable.

Countless are warriors
who face the wrath of their opposition.
Countless are worshipers
who believe in silent contemplation.

What power do I have to describe You
and Your creation?

My powerlessness precludes
even a simple act of sacrifice!

Whatever pleases You
will public good secure.
Glory of the Formless One
shall forever endure.

Meditation 18

Countless are fools
who are appallingly ignorant.
Countless are thieves
who are disgustingly repugnant.

Countless are rulers
who tyrannize.
Countless are tyrants
who terrorize.

Countless are sinners
who have sin in their blood.
Countless are liars
who wander in falsehood.

Countless are wretches
who have impure minds and live in filthy bins.
Countless are slanderers
who will carry the burden of their sins.

Nanak humbly expresses this thought:
My powerlessness precludes
even a simple act of sacrifice!

Whatever pleases You
will public good secure.
Glory of the Formless One
shall forever endure.

Meditation 19

Countless are Your names
and countless Your abodes.
Beyond reach are Your countless worlds
and celestial modes.

To call these simply countless
is a limiting description.
Through words, we chant Your name
and show our devotion.

Through words, we get knowledge
and learn to sing Your praises.
Through words, is recorded
our destiny and its mazes.

Yet these written words are not binding
on the Supreme Deity.
What You decree, we receive
as Your gift to humanity.

All creation is Your manifestation
and without You there is no habitation.
What power do I have to describe You
and Your creation?

My powerlessness precludes
even a simple act of sacrifice!

Whatever pleases You
will public good secure.
Glory of the Formless One
shall forever endure.

Meditation 20

When hands, feet, and body
are covered with slime,
water washes, cleans,
and purifies before time.

When clothes are soiled
and foul smell they emit,
a cake of soap clears the filth
and makes them fit.

When our soul is overlaid
with sin and shame,
it will be cleansed only
by the love of Your name.

Saints and sinners are not made
by being so-called.
Good and bad actions are known
and our future is destined.

As we sow,
so shall we eat.
With divine will, O Nanak,
this journey do we repeat!

Meditation 21

Pilgrimage, atonement,
compassion and creed
will fetch us merit, if any,
tiny as a sesame seed.

By hearing, obeying,
and loving Your name divine,
we purify ourselves
and bathe in the sacred inner shrine.

All virtue resides in You,
and none in me that others can see.
Without virtuous actions,
no one is a true devotee.

My salutation to You,
O Creator of Maya and the sacred word!
Truth and beauty ever reside
in Your blissful heart and word.

What was the occasion, what hour,
what date, and day of the week?
What was the season,
what month did the Creator seek?

Pundit knows not the time,
as it is not mentioned in the Puran.
Kazi knows not the time
after reading the Koran.

Yogi knows not the day, season,
or month of this calendar.
Only the Creator knows the intricacies
of this cosmic grammar.

How should I address, describe,
and know Thee, O love of mine?
O Nanak, we offer discourses
but are unable to properly define!

There is only one Supreme Creator,
who is our sole mover.
O Nanak, the pretentious will not have
much glory to uncover!

Meditation 22

Millions are the lower regions
and countless spaces of unbounded vastness.
Wise ones have searched in vain,
and the Vedas, too, declare helplessness.

Semitic texts count eighteen thousand,
although there is only one essence.
Your infinity no one can measure;
this search is of little consequence.

Only the Divine, O Nanak,
knows the True Self!

Meditation 23

Devotees who worship You
know not Your greatness,
as rivers and rivulets know not
the oceanic vastness.

Kings with wealth greater than
the sweep of an ocean
are worthless if their minds are not
filled with Your devotion.

Meditation 24

Infinite is the measure of divine attributes
and their numbering.
Infinite is the measure of divine actions
and divine giving.

Infinite is the measure of divine perception
and divine listening.
Infinite is the measure of divine mind
and divine thinking.

Infinite is the measure of divine shaping
and divine creating.
Infinite is the dimension of its beginning
and ending.

Many have yearned to know the limits
of divine creation.
Yet this search ended in vain,
without a clue or information.

This limit no one really knows;
the more we say, the greater it shows.

You are the Supreme Being
and Your seat is highest in fame.
Highly praised and exalted
is Your loving name.

If there was someone, just any one,
with Your prime stature,
only then would we know
the meaning of Your vesture.

You are the sole judge and evaluator
of Your greatness.
O Nanak, treasure the gift of God's mercy
and graciousness!

Meditation 25

Your generosity
we cannot in word record.
The Beloved seeks
not a seed we can afford.

Even the mighty seek
Your favor and endearment.
And others, whose numbers
are beyond good judgment.
There are those
who rot in evil encampment.

There are those
who receive without gratitude.
And others,
who consume with servitude.

There are those
who are victims of hunger and chastisement.
But they accept this
as a divine gift of spiritual fulfillment.

Your benevolence
can break our mortal bond.
No one can interfere
with the divine plan, here or beyond.

If any fool ventures
to unfold Your mystery,
unlimited blows will that person receive
for such buffoonery.

You know our needs
and give to us carefully.
Only a few acknowledge this
and live gracefully.

If You be so pleased
to confer Your blessings,
the recipient, O Nanak,
will be the King of Kings!

Meditation 26

Priceless are Your qualities
and measures.
Priceless are Your trades
and treasures.

Priceless are what You provide
and what is taken away.
Priceless are those who are absorbed
in Your love every day.

Priceless are Your law
and the court of corrections.
Priceless are the scales
and weights that measure actions.

Priceless are Your blessings,
marks, and benedictions.
Priceless are Your benevolence
and proclamations.

Priceless, priceless beyond words,
is all that defies expression.
Those who repeat Your name
are immersed in deep devotion.

Vedas and Puranas attempt to explain
Your greatness.
Scholars read this
and proffer their thoughtfulness.

Brahma and Indra attempt
to laud You.
Gopis and Govinda attempt
to praise You.

Shiva and ascetics sing
of You.
Many enlightened souls
acclaim You.

Demons and demigods
revere You.
Demigods and silent meditators
worship You.

Many have said
and more will attempt to say.

Many have spoken
before making their headway.

If You were to create
as many people as already exist,
they will fail to portray
Your greatness, even if we insist.

You are as exalted
as You wish to appear in your fullness.
O Nanak, the True One guards the secret
of Its own greatness!
Someone attempting to describe You
will manifest foolishness.

Meditation 27

Where is the gate,
where is the great mansion?
Where is the place for You
to watch Your creation?

Countless are the instruments
that make divine melodies.
Countless are the songs,
and many are the players of symphonies.

Wind, water, and fire sing praises,
while Dharmaraj keeps appreciating.
Shiva, Brahma, and goddesses laud Thee
with sheer beauty permeating.

Chitra and Gupta keep record,
while Dharmaraj does the adjudicating.
God Indra sings with other godlings,
who also find it truly exciting.

Saints in deep trance chant the Divine Name
in soul nourishing contemplation.
The self-restrained, virtuous, and contented
join in this jubilation.

Scholars and sages laud You
in texts written in many ages.
Mermaids extol You
from upper, lower, and middle stages.

Fourteen sacred objects sing
with sixty-eight sacred places.
Mighty heroes and four sources of life
pay their homages.

There are those who sing
as a sign of their thanksgiving.
There are others, O Nanak,
who are beyond imagining.

You are True and
Supreme Truth is Thy manifestation.
You are and shall remain
the sole Creator of this creation.

Choosing different species and colors,
You made this sensual reality.
Beholding this creation,
You provide testimony to Your immensity.

Your actions are Your pleasure,
restrained by no other demand.
You are, O Nanak, the Supreme Ruler
who is fully in command!

Meditation 28

Take earrings of contentment, and carry
the begging-bowl of honest effort.
Let ashes of awareness embrace your body
as a sign of spiritual support.

Make the awareness of approaching mortality
your patched garment;
let purity be a way of life,
with the staff of faith acting as a deterrent.

Stay closer to like-minded associates
who are from the same upper world.
When you conquer the mind,
you conquer the world.

Let me hail Thee, O Supreme Being!
Without the beginning or the end,
living through all time.

Meditation 29

Let divine knowledge be our nourishment,
compassion our treasure.
Let us listen to the internal melody
to experience true rapture.

You are the real owner
of this vast universe.
Wealth and rituals are diversions,
and even perverse.

Union and separation are
for Deity to arrange.
We receive what our good actions
get in exchange.

Let me hail Thee, O Supreme Being!
Without the beginning or the end,
living through all time.

Meditation 30

The Primal Mother, through a mysterious union,
delivered three sons, known as the holy trinity.
One was the creator, second was the preserver,
and the third was the judge of human frivolity.

In reality, nothing happens without Your will,
O Savior Magnanimous.
Unseen to the trinity, You watch them all,
which is simply marvelous.

Let me hail Thee, O Primal Being!
Without the beginning or the end,
living through all time.

Meditation 31

Your throne and treasures
are in numerous worlds that hold all.
These places were fully
and adequately stocked once and for all.

The Creator, having created the universe,
watches over it.
O Nanak, the maker of Truth,
is Truth explicit.

Let me hail Thee, O Primal Being!
Without the beginning or the end,
living through all time.

Meditation 32

If I had not one but one hundred thousand tongues,
multiplying twentyfold as a simple matter.
A hundred thousand times
would I say Your name with all my power.

Such single-minded devotion
is a ladder that joins me with the Supreme Beloved.
The sound of the celestial song
raises even the lesser worm-like quadruped.

Only divine grace takes us there, O Nanak,
and let false ones boast and be evil-minded!

Meditation 33

I have no power to speak
or keep silent.
I have no power to ask
or be benevolent.

I have no power to live
or die of my own will or action.
I have no power to gain wealth
that causes mental commotion.

I have no power to gain consciousness
or divine knowledge, or to meditate.
I have no power to leave this world
or just to reincarnate.

One who has the power,
will use it as our caretaker.
By our own strength, O Nanak,
no one is a maker or a breaker!

Meditation 34

You made nights,
seasons, lunar days and weekdays.
Air, water, fire,
and infernal walkways.

Installed in the middle is this earth
as a habitat for moral living.
Therein, You created beings
of all colors and shading.

Although they have different names
and infinite identities,
they are judged finally
by their moral proclivities.

You are Supreme Truth,
and true is Your transaction.
You accept and honor those
who really deserve redemption.

Their actions have earned them
a mark of recognition.
The imperfect are separated from the perfect
at this destination.
O Nanak, on reaching there,
we shall know about our selection!

Meditation 35

The moral realm is the realm of moral deeds,
actions, and living.
Thereafter, follows the realm of knowledge,
which is quite amazing.

There are primal elements keeping company
with gods of extreme sacredness.
There are divine craftsmen crafting the universe
with different shades of loveliness.

There are fields of righteous action,
meditations of Dhruv on Meru Mountain.
There are abodes of Indra,
moons, suns, and the entire solar domain.

There are abodes of sages, seers,
and goddesses of utmost devotion.
There are demons, demigods,
and jewels churned out of oceanic commotion.

There are sources of creation,
forms of speech, and people of royal connection.
Countless, O Nanak, are the enlightened ones,
and there is no count of their reflection!

Meditation 36

In the realm of divine knowledge,
there is an explosion of spiritual enlightenment.
There are mystic melodies
filling hearts with joy and discernment.

In the realm of spiritual beauty,
there is an unfoldment of incomparable forms.
Many splendid shapes are crafted here,
which defy the usual norms.

The dramatic events in this realm,
if described, will look awkward.
Anyone who tries to say
will repent afterward.

Over here, soul consciousness, intellect, and emotions
are finely blended.
Miraculous powers of great seers
are divinely extended.

Meditation 37

In the realm of divine grace,
You are Supreme and the spirit is pure.
Unless it is desired, nothing else
resides here for sure.

There live warriors, heroes
of great spiritual strength.
Their hearts are immersed in the Divine Name
in all its breadth and length.

And there are celestial goddesses,
maidens, and beauties most divine.
Their graceful looks our words
can hardly define.

They do not die or get deluded
by the limits of their own mental confines.
Their hearts are forever filled
with the sacred love of Divine's.

There live devotees,
who belong to different solar regions.
They are in an eternal bliss,
cherishing the True One's beauteous visions.

In the realm of eternal truth
lives the formless Supreme Being,
whose glance of one loving grace
is a source of joy and yearning.

There are lands, regions,
and biospheres we are unable to comprehend.
If we start describing them,
we shall never reach the end.

There are myriad worlds upon worlds
in perfect alignment,
all wholly subservient, and acting precisely
as per Your commandment.

What You see brings You happiness,
but what You contemplate,
O Nanak, is as hard as steel
to narrate!

Meditation 38

Make self-restraint your oven
and cultivate a master goldsmith's tenderness.
Be informed by an awakened mind
and sharpen the tools of your consciousness.

Let our Beloved's name be the bellows
and atonement be the heat and fire.
In this crucible of love, forge oneness
with the One for whom you aspire.

Fulfillment comes to those
who are blessed with divine grace.
O Nanak, through our Beloved's loving glance,
we attain everlasting blissful grace.

Epilogue

Air, the Preceptor; water, the Father;
and earth, the Mother.
Day and night are our nurses,
and we grow in the lap of a foster mother.

Our good and bad actions will be examined
by an impartial judge in true earnestness.
Some of us will be divinely embraced,
while others will fall farther into darkness.

Those who worship the Name
will have their suffering terminated.
O Nanak, with their faces glowing, they
and their loved ones will be emancipated!

Part Two

Japji

Explanatory Notes on Meditations

Japji
Explanatory Notes on Meditations

Prologue

In the name of the One True Supreme Being,
who is the Creator of all other beings,
without fear and hatred;
of timeless form,
unborn, self-existent;
attainable
only through divine grace!

Japji begins with a *mool* mantra, which is a beautiful statement of Guru Nanak's fundamental belief about the nature of God and our relationship with the Supreme. "One True Supreme Being" is a powerful affirmation of the unity of God. The specific qualities of God, such as truth, fearlessness, timelessness, and formlessness, reinforce the conception of One God as explained below.

Truth is equated with God, as truth is the very essence of God. Human conception of truth is often tainted by our own limited vision of what is right or wrong. Therefore, truth is something relative to our existence and our experiences. We are unable to see the ultimate truth or the eternal order that God has created for us. The eternal truth is beyond our imagination and understanding. For God, there is no duality because in God's presence everything manifests itself as unity. Everything unfolds its true nature; there is no possibility of any false appearance because God sees the true essence of everything. There are no half-truths in this realm; either something exists in its true essence or not at all. There is nothing that is relative in the sense of being true, subject to the existence of other causal factors. In the divine presence, there is no other causality.

God is beyond all fear. Fear is the product of our ego-mind and our dependence on the external world. Spiritual energy, being pure consciousness, is above ego. We are unable to see the inner reality, in view of our enslavement by our ego-mind. The ego creates fear because it also creates attachments. When we are attached to other people and things, we have to learn to live with the fear of losing them. This creates insecurity, which in turn leads to more fear, including the biggest fear of all, the fear of dying.

God is above malice, which is a human tendency born in the absence of love. If we completely fill ourselves with love and develop the strength to practice love as the sole principle of living, we can get rid of hatred. People who immerse their identities in the divine name shall be free from all fears and feelings of hatred.

God is loving and merciful. Creation is the work of God's love and compassion. We have been given a rare opportunity to participate in the wonders of this magical universe. The creation is so vast and so varied that the Creator could be nothing but a fountain of love and compassion for all living beings. We would not be able to live without fresh air that rejuvenates us at all times. We would not be able to quench our thirst without fresh, clean water. We would have nothing to eat without fertile soil. The merciful and loving

God provided this for us and we need to preserve this gift of love.

In reality, human beings have not been very good custodians and caretakers. We have filled the air with noxious fumes. We have polluted the rivers and streams with toxic substances. We have burned and destroyed forests. We have denuded the soil of its nutrients. And we continue to indulge in acts of destruction and vandalism that harm the global environment. We do this because we have forgotten that these natural assets are God's creation and gift.

God is formless and timeless. We are able to identify ourselves easily with a personal God who we imagine looks like a human being. It is difficult, however, to picture a formless God, a presence without an appearance. Yet it is important to understand that God's visible manifestation cannot be limited to a form and a shape that belongs only to the human race, which is but one among several billion species created by God.

The idea of formlessness cannot be separated from the idea of timelessness. Anything that is limited to a given form cannot be timeless. The Guru presents a conception of God that modern science, in particular quantum physics, has uncovered only in this century. Everything we see or touch is made up of matter that can be subdivided into subatomic particles. This division follows an endless rhythm, its ultimate limits have not been reached by even the most advanced science. Based on what we know, it is clear that tiniest particles move in an empty space, which in relative terms is equal to the distance of one galaxy from another. Within this visible body of ours there is an empty space that cannot be measured in precise terms, even with the most sophisticated scientific instruments. Yet all of us are proud of our form, our body and its physical attributes. We are totally unaware of our own formlessness.

The formless God is the energy that powers everything—meteors, glaciers, tropical forests, koala bears, human beings. God, as a subtle form of energy, is present in everything and everywhere. Places of worship are convenient outlets for us to get in touch with God, but there is no place and no being that is away from God's love at any time. In order for us to experience this presence, we have to develop our capacity to see something that we do not ordinarily see and to hear the voice that is not normally audible to our ears. What we do not see is the presence of a formless God, and the voice that we do not hear, in fact, is the divine melody hidden in the depths of our hearts.

God is unincarnated, self-existent, self-generating, and immortal. Humans have none of these attributes. Our mortality is predetermined. Our life is like a journey of self-realization, of finding meaning in what we are and using the power of the Name to attain a state of bliss after this life—our union with a loving God. The Creator has no need to go through the process of living and dying. The Supreme was present before the creation and will be there long after creation has ceased to be. God is not limited by this world as we know it. God's worlds and realms are beyond our reckoning. Death is a requirement for us; it is in reality a ladder for our enlightenment. Living this life is essential for us because it is only during this life that our soul gets an opportunity to express itself, to explore its potential, and to find a direction beyond the reach of this life.

God is also the Supreme Preceptor, the greatest spiritual guide, mentor, and teacher of all. This is the manifest form of God. But this manifestation does not take the form of an avatar, a god in visible form. God is an inner experience open to all human beings, irrespective of their status in life. Preceptor, in this sense, is the holy word that helps us attain our spiritual goals.

Meditation 1

Meditate.

You were True
at the beginning
and in the primal age.
Says Nanak of the Supreme,
You are True
and You will ever remain True!

We cannot gain understanding
through monotonous contemplation.
True silence is not attained
through trance-like meditation.

Neither through worldly possessions
is our hunger appeased,
nor through a million other mental feats
is enlightenment achieved.

How to prove our truth before You
and lift the veil of darkness?
Only submission to the divine order,
O Nanak, can give us awareness!

The word "meditate" (*jap*) at the start of this first meditation lends itself to more than one interpretation. First, it suggests a title for this whole set of meditations. Second, it is a command to recite the Name and to immerse ourselves in the meditations that follow. Third, it helps us to get into a truly meditative mood. *Japji,* in its essence, is an invitation to honor, celebrate, recite, and internalize this creation and, through this celebration, advance the momentum of our own spiritual evolution.

We are reminded of God's existence when time was not measured in the way we measure it now. Our concept of time starts with the "big bang," the starting point for planetary evolution, and it will end with the "big crunch," the starting point for the universe to commence material contraction. God has lived through the known as well as unknown segments of geologic time and will continue to live beyond this visible reality. This means that God is beyond time, and the divine presence in this universe transcends any quantitative measurement known to us.

Intellectual or meditative pursuits are necessary but not sufficient conditions to unravel the great mystery of our being and our relationship with God. The material world is inadequate to satisfy our spiritual cravings. Rational thinking is equally deficient. We need to realize that we are governed by the divine order, which is an expression of the will of God. This is not a scientific puzzle or a clever gimmick. Everything is divinely ordained. Nothing happens by chance. By submitting our will to the will of God, we enlarge the area of our awareness, an awareness that brings us true freedom.

In this meditation, we are introduced to the concept of the divine order. We may harbor illusions about our own physical and spiritual powers: we think we can attain enlightenment through our own efforts. In reality, what we need is a total submission to the divine command. Only through the process of total submission can we ensure that the atonement we seek will come our way. Thinking, itself, will not help us because our mind is limited in terms of its ability to fully comprehend the idea of God. No clever schemes or devices will work; what is needed is an acceptance of the Name as the final and only arbiter of our destiny.

We have to give unconditional love to obtain unconditional love from our Supreme Beloved. Seeking material
things makes for conditional love. The veil of darkness that
surrounds us symbolizes our ignorance of our position on
this planet, not knowing where we are coming from and
where we are going. Once this veil is lifted, our life is suddenly illuminated by a glow of divine love. Then we can
see ourselves as spiritual beings and understand how the
entire existence is divinely guided. Our journey is not a
chance happening. It is the continuation of our yearning to
lead a life of eternal bliss. This awareness should bring us
closer to our true freedom—a freedom to realize the fullest
potential of our soul being.

Meditation 2

Divine order that creates life
is not easy to name.
Divine order that gives life
confers honor and fame.

Divine order makes us high or low,
happy or sad again.
Divine grace saves some,
others live and are born again.

Divine order encompasses
and rules us all.
O Nanak, believers have
no ego-mind at all!

This meditation is a celebration of the divine order and divine grace. Whatever experiences we get in life—happiness,
joy and sorrow—are the gradual unfoldment of the order
that supersedes everything else. From the pain of the separation to the bliss of the union, these are gifts that our Supreme Beloved has assembled for us. We should live and
enjoy every moment. The fire that burns inside us is our

prayer, our meditation. Not even for a moment should we be blindly driven by our ego-mind. Our existence itself is the glorious and generous act of our Creator.

As a creator of this universe, God makes it possible for various life forms or species to be born. The enormous variety of animals, birds, fish, and plants, known as biodiversity, is testimony to the limitless imagination of the maker to conceive such myriad forms and to infuse them with the gift of life. Such a creator is beyond expression in words. We can imagine the utter sublimity and grandeur of God, but are unable to ascribe meaning to this scheme of things.

All honors and rewards can be traced back to the divine order. That is why it is important to remember that truly blessed are those who live with the full realization of the absolute authority of God. This thought is central to their very existence; not even for a second do they forget their need to totally submit to the dictates of God. Lest it sound somewhat authoritarian, we need to remember that God is not a despot. God is the source of all caring and nurturing. By submitting ourselves to God's command, we submit ourselves to the constant flow of love that fills our body and soul with grace, compassion, unity, and immortality.

Quite often, we take pride in our worldly achievements. But the real achievement comes with divine grace. Our life is a roller coaster of highs and lows, moments of happiness and sadness. We should not be too happy when we are at the peak, and we should not be too disheartened when we hit the ground. We need to remember that everything that happens to us has a divine purpose. If we lead a life of prayer and meditation, there is nothing for us to worry about. In the midst of happiness or pain, we can enjoy moments of bliss, provided we continue to follow the right path.

Our life is painful because it is part of the eternal life and death cycle. Our birth is a traumatic event. Our life is full of pain and suffering because we never fully achieve what we want. In the end, we lose what is precious to us: positions of power and authority, comforts and riches, friends and relatives. In every dark alley in our life there is the shadow of death, the fear of being crippled and incapacitated. The only way for us to get out of this cycle of life and death is to seek atonement, to elevate our life to a higher plane of consciousness where we conquer our ego and submerge our identity in the ocean of love that surrounds us, but whose presence we tend to ignore.

The divine order extends to all beings without any exception. The powerful among us entertain illusions of immortality, thinking they can use deceit and cunning. By the time they realize their folly, it is generally too late. Worldly possessions and vestiges of worldly power stay behind us; we have to move forward on our eternal journey only with our good deeds. The Guru warns us that we must shed our false pride and self-centeredness and submit ourselves to the divine order if we seek salvation from the cycles of pain and suffering.

Meditation 3

Those who have the depth of understanding,
they sing of Your grace and benefaction.
Those who know Your noble attributes,
they sing of Your knowledge and deep absorption.

Those who know of Your ability to create and destroy,
they sing of Your gift of renewal and regeneration.
While some sing of Your detachment and distance,
others sing of Your omnipresence and attention.

There is no end to our praise and our description;
millions have sung Your praises with veneration.

You give to us untiringly, but the recipients get wearied;
through the ages, we have lived on Your benediction.

The movement of this universe is divinely willed.
O Nanak, there is self-realization and perfection!

There are many ways to praise God. People look at one facet and they are carried away. In reality, there are countless dimensions of the Supreme Being, with no inherent contradictions. If we open our eyes with love, we shall see the most beautiful vision—always generous, encouraging, forgiving, and nudging us to move forward. We should accept the totality of this vision, submitting ourselves to the will of the Creator.

This meditation presents different human perceptions of God. Some people are impressed by the power at God's command. For them, God is the source of immense might to create and to destroy. This perception results in fear. Other people look upon God as the source of all knowledge and learning. Some are swayed by God's life-giving and life-destroying attributes. There are those who think that God is very detached, far removed from the rough and tumble of their daily lives. And there are those, although a minority, who think that they are never absent from divine love and compassion.

Paradoxical although it might appear, God is all these things and more. In fact, human imagination can never find limits to divine manifestations. There are no limits to God's generosity. God controls a treasury of gifts that is far beyond our imagination. We can tire of receiving an endless chain of gifts, but the Creator knows no end to the care and nurture of this vast creation of which we are an integral part.

There is freedom to choose our relationship with our Supreme Beloved, based on our own preferences: as a mighty force, as a benevolent being, as a source of wisdom, or as a creator and destroyer of life. But we have no freedom to ignore the fact that the divine order will prevail under all circumstances. It is only through this realization that we can find meaning and purpose in our life.

Meditation 4

The True One's name is repeated
with boundless affection.
Those who ask for gifts,
receive endless benediction.

What can we offer
for a glimpse of the court divine?
What prayer can we offer
to receive Your love pristine?

When dawn breaks,
we sing glories of Your greatness.
Although karma influences,
liberation is attained with divine graciousness.

O Nanak, be it known:
the True One is the fountain of truthfulness!

The embodiment of truth speaks to us in the language of love. As human beings, we have some understanding of love and its manifestations, but divine love is much deeper and sweeter than the love we experience in our daily lives. The rain shower of our Beloved's love, when experienced, is the ultimate joy of peace, compassion, beauty, and bliss at the same time. It is love that accepts no boundaries. Bounded love is a typical human fallacy, dependent on other conditions being satisfied by its recipient. Divine love knows no beginning or end. Once we receive it, it will stay with us forever; our path will shine, and our journey beyond this life will be smooth on the pathways that connect life with death.

Once we realize that God is a generous giver of valuable gifts, we may raise our demands. We can ask for things of material value. We can ask for gifts of happiness for ourselves and for those whom we love. We may want things to happen here and now. This is not a problem. For the generous dispenser of love and happiness, no demand is really too big. But the question is how do we repay our debt? Material offerings could have only symbolic meaning because matter has no permanent value, other than being a speck in the cosmic dust. The way to fulfill our obligations is to open our hearts and minds to our Beloved's presence. We should engross ourselves in meditation of the Name.

It is known that our birth in this life is determined by our past actions or karma. Karma, or predestination, is the law of dynamic causation and interaction between the higher and lower levels of our being. As the soul goes through a variety of experiences, we can reach a higher level if our actions in this life so warrant. In the soul's journey through time, we can accumulate rewards for good deeds. In the same way, our wrong doings can demote us on our evolutionary path. As long as our lower nature remains active, we continue to incur karmic deeds. But this is not simple causation, nor is it a simple game of chance.

This meditation combines karmic results with the most important need for grace. When everything is counted, our liberation from the cycles of life and death depends on divine grace. Good actions alone are not sufficient. They can pave the way, but unless we fill our life with the love of God and submit ourselves to the divine order there can be no release and enlightenment.

Meditation 5

Neither installed nor crafted by skill,
You are immaculate and self-existent.

Those who serve You are truly meritorious.
O Nanak, sing praises of the magnificent!

Sing and hear the glories of the One
who takes away misery and gives fulfillment.
The sound of the sacred word is divine knowledge,
and the word itself is all-pervasive and resplendent.

God is Shiva, Vishnu, and Brahma;
Goddess is Parvati, Lakshmi, and Sarasvati.

Even if I understand the True One,
how do I describe Thee?

The Guru gave me one advice:
there is one God of all creation,
let me not forget.

This meditation reminds us of God's true nature. Being form-less, shapeless, and self-creating, God is free from constraints that bind us and limit our potential as human beings. We have a form that we inherit at birth. We are self-creating only in a limited sense. We can grow only within the boundaries of our own potential. God is beyond any limitations, truly self-generating in the sense of transcending all material manifestations.

Meditation of the Name is not only an obligation, it is also an honor. Blessed are the souls who are so evolved that they are able to recite the Name. Lowly creatures and human beings at the lower end of their spiritual evolution are not so blessed. They are unaware of the pleasure that is available to those who recite the Name. True devotees are unaffected by the pangs of sorrows that can break the spirit of ordinary folks. They not only experience happiness on their own, but they also spread it around. Imagine the effect that the presence of a God-loving person has on his or her environment. Rays of light seem to emanate from the pores of such a person. The air gets lighter and fragrant. Good thoughts pack the air with their intensity and depth of meaning. Hatred, malice, selfishness, and other negative energies evaporate into thin air. This is the magic of divine love.

When we carry a divine aura around us or meet someone who is divinely blessed, we can experience a sudden change in our surroundings. This is why people recite holy prayers at the time of sickness or death of their dear ones. When the Name is uttered, no evil spirit can stay around. Eternal peace prevails. The pain of sickness can be reduced or totally eliminated. The path of the dying person thus can be cleared.

This meditation refers to the trinity of gods: Brahma, Vishnu, and Shiva. Shiva is the destroyer (destruction being a stage in the process of creation) and in many respects is the god of gods (Mahadeva). Vishnu is the preserver and, in this role, is the embodiment of the qualities of mercy and goodness. Brahma is the creator of the universe, the god of wisdom, and the guardian of the Vedas. Parvati, who is Shiva's consort and female energy, is Mother Durga, who in another incarnation destroys Mahisha, the demon who threatened to dispossess the gods. Lakshmi, as the consort of Vishnu, was reborn once as one of the fourteen precious jewels from the churning of the milk ocean. In modern times, she has been worshipped on her own as the goddess who brings affluence and prosperity. Sarasvati, as the consort of Brahma, is the goddess of poetry, music, and higher learning. She is also the great linguist who invented the Sanskrit language.

Although these gods and goddesses appear separate and are even worshipped separately, they are creations of one God. This message of universal love and unity consciousness is essential for our enlightenment as human beings. We spend too much time and energy in pursuing separate paths and making each path look different; we ignore the fact that all spiritual paths lead to the same destination.

The spiritual endeavor is also an attempt at self-realization. Sacred words are essential at the start of the journey because we need to visualize the process of self-transformation. But once we are far ahead in our pursuits, we are gripped by an overbearing passion of divine love. It starts living in our thoughts and recollections. Every breath is sanctified by the presence of our Beloved. Every action is guided by clear light. Our entire being is transformed by the intensity of our goal-driven emotions.

Meditation 6

Holy bathing is fruitless
if Your pleasure is not obtained.
Divine creation that I behold
is not without destiny attained.

With Your guidance,
the hidden mental treasure is regained.

My Preceptor gave me one advice:
there is one God of all creation,
let me not forget.

This meditation explains the importance of grace and our true potentiality. The traditional religions of India prescribe taking a sacred journey to bathe in holy rivers. Although this is easy, particularly for people who have the money to go on such trips, there is no guarantee that these actions by themselves are sufficient to be rewarding in any manner. And if the Supreme is not pleased, they are wasteful efforts.

If we sincerely desire atonement, we have to make an effort greater than simply making ritualistic offerings. It calls for intense concentration and meditation. It entails remembrance of the Name. It means setting high moral standards for our life. Being and doing are inseparable. What is required is a perfect alignment between our personal and public behaviors. God sees through all falsehood. Keeping an outward appearance of piety is meaningless.

There is a reference in this meditation to human potential. Hidden inside all of us is a container holding the treasury of jewels (our potential). These jewels are much more precious than those we know and value. The hidden jewels symbolize our divinity and our ability to ask for and to receive God's love. God has not given up on this creation; we have forgotten God in our attempt to gain worldly power, fame, and fortune. Even those who commit serious crimes have the potential to ask for forgiveness. It is never too late to get back on the right path. But this cannot happen until we become conscious of our own true potential.

Because the hidden treasure is hard to reach when it is covered by weeds, our hidden treasure is inaccessible if we allow the dust of our actions to settle on it. Of course, there is always time, and we could postpone this discovery to our last day. But prayer in that case is self-serving. God sees and weighs our intentions on the scales of eternity before giving us another chance to redeem ourselves. We can cross the gulf between death and immortality if we ceaselessly work for it.

Meditation 7

Even if our life span
covers four ages times ten.
Even if we gain
nine continents, with all souls beholden.

Even if our good name and deeds
have won us worldly recognition.
Without Your blessing and grace,
all this adds up to pure indiscretion.

We will be the lowest of all beings
and notoriously infamous.

O Nanak, the unmerited can gain true merit
and become truly virtuous!

But is there any one
who can bestow any virtue on You?

We pray for long life. But how long could our life span actually be? This meditation suggests a limit of four ages times ten. What is the significance of four ages? According to Hindu mythology, Brahma creates the universe, and it takes one full day of four and one-third million years to do the job. When the work of creation is done, Brahma sleeps for a period that lasts an equal amount of time; the universe is manifested and it runs its course in four ages or yugas. These are *krita* (the golden age, lasting nearly two million years), *treta* (lasting nearly one million years, in which virtue already is starting to disappear), *dwapara* (lasting less than one million years, in which virtue is only half present), and *kali* (the present age of degeneration, which started at Krishna's death and will last less than one-half million years; it is marked by slavery, degradation, oppression, famines, and wars).

The *kali-yuga,* or the age of Kali, will end with the coming of the Kalki—the tenth and last incarnation of Vishnu—who will destroy the wicked and prepare the ground for renewal of creation. Then Shiva will come out of his cave to do *tandav* (the greatest dance of all) that destroys the universe.

Since each of these ages consists of thousands of years, living for this length of time is beyond any stretch of imagination. Even if it is possible to have our life spread over such vast periods of time, it would not serve any useful purpose. What could be the purpose of such a life if it is devoid of divine love? Clearly, what is important is not the length of time we actually live but what we do with our life. A short life filled with divine love is worth more than a long life lived in pursuit of other things.

The meditation draws our attention to the fallacy of fame and wealth. It is not bad to be rich or famous. In fact, only those who are divinely blessed have material abundance in life. Riches and fame should not distract us from living a meditative life. Once we start accepting material things as the sole end of our life, however, spiritual degeneration becomes inevitable. A life free from God's presence is truly worthless; it would be a diversion from our main goal. It is the kind of life that is led by creatures at the lower end of the evolutionary scale.

The choices we make are important because the choice of being nearer to God is open to all of us. Our past actions do not stand in the way of renewing ourselves. God gives us freedom to start all over again at every juncture of our life. We can hear the call if we have sharpened our perception of differentiating the real from the unreal.

Meditation 8

Hearing Your name
makes one a spiritually realized being and a yogi.
Hearing Your name
reveals this earth, a mythical bull, and the sky.

Hearing Your name,
we know hidden worlds and regions.
Hearing Your name,
we conquer death's legions.

O Nanak, devotees ever are
in a blissful state!
Hearing Your name,
our sorrows and sins negate.

When we hear a prayer, we remember God and our senses are filled with spiritual energy. Remembrance is not only a memory that comes alive; it is a feast for our body, mind, and soul. It is total transformation. We witness the miracle of unfolding mysteries, including mythological revelations such as the earth being kept in balance on the horns of a bull. We overcome the fear of death. We attain bliss experienced by a true yogi. Just this one act of hearing the Name makes our sins disappear. The Name should be the starting point of our meditation. It is no ordinary name; it conveys the qualities of omnipresence and omniscience. Hearing the Name is also remembrance.

Remembrance of God does not necessarily involve painful meditation in lonely places. There is a simple meditation that is equally effective: hearing or reciting the Name. Any place or any time is good for it. Such is the power and beauty of God's name that even lending our ears to it could make a difference. We could gain wisdom, saintliness, and contentment. If hearing the Name is so profitable, we can imagine what rewards would come our way if we could dedicate our life to the pursuit of this goal.

Hearing the Name has other benefits, too, those relating to our bonds with the external world, the natural world, and the vastness of empty spaces that have no visible boundaries. Our body is so small compared with the vastness that surrounds us. This should not worry us because we do not stand apart from the earth and the sky above us. What is within us—our subatomic structure—is also what is outside. But the realization of this unity could come only through the power of the Name. When we hear the Name, it is also heard by other beings, stones, particles, and matter, elements that are in perpetual motion in the cosmic vastness. It is the Name that binds us to the rest of the universe. We are no longer small, isolated, insignificant beings. We become partners in the magic of creation.

Hearing the Name puts us in touch with what is below the surface of this earth: infernal regions that are symbolic of the underworld, or four lower planes of nature where Greek gods, such as Pluto, rule. This is the region that is commonly associated with hell, hades, or sheol. This is not only a place for tormenting lower level beings but also for purifying them in the eternal fires that burn there all the time. We need have no fear of these regions and hell fires because, if we hear the Name, we shall be purified without these fires.

The Name frees us from fears of all kinds. We are no longer afraid of the power of tyrants, ugly beasts, or ghosts. The Name gives us our true freedom. A life without fear is a life filled with the love of God. Hearing the Name makes God dwell within us. We are blessed from within. Sorrow and pain cannot touch us ever again.

Meditation 9

Hearing Your name,
we are like Shiva, Brahma, and Indra transformed.
Hearing Your name,
even lower beings are divinely ordained.

Hearing Your name,
we understand the body's secrets.
Hearing Your name,
we acquire spiritual secrets.

O Nanak, devotees ever are
in a blissful state!
Hearing Your name,
our sorrows and sins negate.

Inner transformation can occur through meditation. We can develop within ourselves the power and spiritual reach of gods and goddesses. In a truly blissful state, pain and suffering do not affect us. When we think of God, we see the glorious manifestation of sublime beauty in everything. Ordinary human beings can attain total transformation if they recite the Name. Shiva, Brahma, and Indra are symbols of divine power. Shiva enjoys a distinctive place in Hindu mythology, in view of his many roles as a fearsome destroyer, lover, and ascetic, but he is very often a quarrelsome deity. Brahma is the creator of the universe and, as such, he is first among all the gods. He is also the god of wisdom and the wellspring of the Vedas. Indra is a god of storms and thunderbolts that he uses to destroy the demons. He also brings rain, which is essential for human survival and prosperity.

One could imagine the combined sweep of celestial power that these deities possess. We might wonder about the insignificance of an ordinary human being, compared with these powerful deities. Yet these gods are used as metaphors for extraordinary power that could be attained if we embrace the purity, beauty, and sublimity of the Name.

It is generally believed that God's compassion is reserved for the virtuous and the truthful. Those who lead sinful lives, commit murders, and torment other human beings, and those who live for themselves and have hearts devoid of any feelings for the suffering of others, are not worthy of divine compassion. This meditation presents another viewpoint. Human beings are worthy of divine mercy at any time of their lives, provided they change themselves, give up a life of greed and lust, and genuinely pray for atonement.

An active listener is one who absorbs the purity of the holy word and allows oneself to be transformed into a new person. A passive listener, on the other hand, does not make any effort and is possibly still numbed by worldly desires. For an active listener, hearing the Name by itself brings out the hidden magic. We are no longer limited physically or hopelessly tyrannized by our own karma. The Name gives back to us our freedom to attain our higher potential, and we are gradually raised to a level where we become worthy of divine praise reserved for gods, like Shiva, Brahma, and Indra.

The Name not only grants us divine merit, it unfolds secrets of our inner being. One reason we act indifferently toward our soul and its needs is that we are unaware of our own spiritual possibilities. We know ourselves as desiring beings, and we know ourselves for our shortcomings like anger, violence, greed, and self-centeredness. We ignore the fact that we are also pure souls, informed and guided by God at every stage in our life. To be unaware of this divine presence is a sin of ignorance.

The source of ultimate wisdom lies in our scriptures, our sacred traditions, and religious texts. It is our duty to gain this wisdom and benefit fully from it. This life is an opportunity to gaining enlightenment. But we need help to muddle through the paths of our own actions. If we are not ready to take the first step, the rest of the way is closed for us. It is only through hearing the inner voice that we can gain momentum to go farther on this path.

Meditation 10

Hearing Your name, we gain truth,
contentment, and discernment.
Hearing Your name equals bathing
at sixty-eight places of sacrament.

Hearing Your name
brings veneration and admiration.
Hearing Your name,
we attain poised meditation.

O Nanak, devotees ever are
in a blissful state!
Hearing Your name,
our sorrows and sins negate.

The expression of love for God is a great transformational act. We can see the difference it makes in our life. It is like making a confession: when we live for ourselves, happiness eludes us. When we live for the world, we are stranded alone, and we are lied to and cheated by our fellow beings. Now, when we live for the love of our Beloved, we know only goodness. Nothing passes by this great source of light without being transformed.

Human existence can be viewed along a spectrum of darkness and light. At lower levels, we are totally devoid of truth, contentment, and discernment or right perception. There are people who have no reservations about lying. They lie or cheat to achieve their objectives, notwithstanding the damage their lies or cheating would do to their victims. Because lies are difficult to disprove, these people can even portray themselves as "victims," deserving of sympathy.

Liars have one thing in common, however: they live in perpetual spiritual darkness. They lead miserable lives, unaware of their misery, the true misery of their souls. Yet they are capable of dragging themselves out of this darkness by subjecting themselves to a new routine in their lives. When they move to the other side of the spectrum, they are informed by truth, contentment, and right perception.

It is common for people to perform ritualistic acts as a measure of self-purification. They seek forgiveness by subjecting themselves to enormous physical inconvenience, such as by traveling to faraway places. This meditation shows us the right way to seek atonement, which does not involve any journey or ritual or financial expense. It requires us to hear the Name with devotion and single-mindedness. We do not have to leave our home to go anywhere because God is omnipresent. If we cannot find the object of our love in our own place, we will not find it anywhere.

Divinity brings us wisdom. In every society, wise people are respected. Those who have attained wisdom are keenly followed, because other people wish to share their wisdom and want to listen to what they have to say. Such admiration must be accepted with great humility. Because we are not perfect, admiration often inflates our egos, and we may make claims of saintliness while we are still mired in the world of desire. In the end, all honor belongs to God. Those who show this understanding will be remembered as true devotees.

Another attribute of wisdom is scholarly distinction. To undertake scholarly work requires much effort; it requires several years of education, followed by specialization in a scientific discipline. Irrespective of the subject of study, all scholarly pursuits are divinely inspired. People who change the world for better through their work are acting as divine agents. Without divine inspiration, no new discovery can be made. True scientists know the limits of tools used to test new hypotheses. They appreciate God's grand design for the universe and for its beings, as reflected in Einstein's famous quip, "God does not play dice."

Hearing the Name is important for all of us—for people who do manual work or those who create new scientific knowledge. True achievement awaits only those who work with humility and pursue their work as a form of meditation. If we forget the sacred Name, our labor could be instrumental in creating a gas chamber or weapons of mass destruction. In all of human history, tyrants were empowered to commit acts of brutality by people who used their craft in ways that were not consistent with divine purposes. This continues to happen today. That is why this message is of such immediate relevance.

The meditation reminds us again about the everlasting bliss that awaits those who are able to absorb the Name. They are saved from suffering and sin. In divine custody, there is only one state of being: true and everlasting bliss.

Meditation 11

Hearing Your name makes one open
a spiritually enriching theme.
Hearing Your name makes one illuminated
Spiritual Guide and Supreme.

Hearing Your name makes the spiritually blind
find their worldly way.
Hearing Your name, fathomless deep truths
come under our sway.

O Nanak, devotees ever are
in a blissful state!
Hearing Your name,
our sorrows and sins negate.

As one of the finest creations of God, human beings are fundamentally empowered to be virtuous. The sacred within us does not easily admit evil in any form. But for several practical reasons, we are quick to lose touch with our divinity. Once this starts to happen, we accept in principle that an accommodation with evil is possible. The worldly attractions, coupled with the power of our ego-mind, are such that we allow the ocean of virtue within us to diminish. Our eyes then cannot see the true self that is within us. The internal eye to see virtue's ocean has to be developed anew through a slow and arduous process of atonement. We have to hear the Name to unravel the mystery of our hidden self.

The hearing process implied here is not passive. Some people believe that hearing means lending our ears to something—the external stimuli pouring into our head. That is not the kind of hearing that is suggested here. Hearing means listening and learning. Listening implies that auditory input impels us to search for meaning, thereby awakening our mental abilities to differentiate one meaning from another. It also implies that we use our heart as well as our mind, logic as well as intuition. The mind alone, as the center of our rational self, lacks the emotional energy to understand the spiritual and mystical undertones of the sacred message. Therefore, we have to listen with our heart as well as our mind. We have to capture the meaning as well as the mystery of the message.

Listening to the Name gives us wisdom. It is not the wisdom of being worldly wise but the wisdom of knowing the ultimate reality, the wisdom that will eventually bring us closer to enlightenment. The reference is to the wisdom of great shaikhs and pirs, in the mystical Sufi tradition. Sufis are known to practice *zikr*, meaning remembrance, which involves chanting the name of God as part of their prayer and meditation. Through this process, they experience the extinction of their ego *(fana)*, which occurs when the mystic attains a perfect union with God. The difference between "I" and "Thou" disappears and the self becomes part of the divine. As the Sufi poet, Rumi, said, "Without putting ourselves out of the way, what do you expect to accomplish?"

When we recite the Name, the voice comes from within. In a way, we are listening to our own voice. But this is no ordinary voice; it is the voice wrapped within a great mystery. The awareness of what is within and what is outside starts to disappear as we reach deeper meditative states. Slowly and gradually, we learn to put ourselves out of the way and merge into the cosmic cycle that connects our ordinary self with the universal consciousness.

Listening to the Name enables us to overcome our blindness. Again, the meditation does not refer to a physical condition, although miracles do happen to cure physical ailments. This blindness is the blindness of the soul, our inability to see the spiritual nature of our being and our potential to attain higher levels of consciousness. Only when we overcome our spiritual blindness are we really able to see. This will happen when we start listening to the Name and start abiding by its discipline.

Listening to the Name, we shall come to know both fathomable and unfathomable mysteries of our existence. The fathomable part of our self is easier to know. It is like knowing our conscious mind. The unfathomable part is much deeper; to find it, we have to delve not only into our "personal unconscious" but into the unknown mysteries of the "collective unconscious," as explained by the Swiss psychologist, Carl Jung. The unfathomable space is the seat or center of our soul. To be in touch with this is to reach the core of our spiritual being—the highest ambition we can carry in our heart.

Listening to the Name confers special blessings. We can live in an everlasting blissful state. Such is the power of the Name that suffering of all kinds and sinful actions disappear. Where there is the Name, there is no suffering. Where there is the Name, there cannot be sin. Our suffering is caused by our moving away from God, indulging ourselves in the world of desire, wealth, and fame driven by our ego-mind. In these pursuits, mental stress is bound to be our companion because we do not wish to fail. We stretch ourselves to the limits of our physical and mental capacities, and then one day the chord breaks. It breaks because there is nothing to support it. The glue of the Name can bind us to our central reality, so that even when we are pursuing our worldly goals we will not be far away from the eternal bliss.

Meditation 12

A believer's bliss
is hard to relate.
All our efforts
will surely negate.

There is no paper,
pen, or penmanship
to describe the believer's bliss
and worship.

Such is the power
of Your immaculate denomination,
that we know it
only through total submission.

The state of self-realization (oneness with Supreme Self) is hard to describe because it is an experience that transcends all human sensory experiences. Any such attempt will be futile because what we have not yet experienced cannot be captured in words. Words can easily miscommunicate and misinform, not so much by conscious design as from the sheer inadequacy of the language itself. An experience is always more intense than its expression.

What is written on paper is an outward expression of an inner state. No pen has the power to write down words that accurately reflect the emotional state of a true follower. The scholarship needed to capture the essence of such experience cannot be cultivated. It has to be divinely gifted. The only true test is the unshakable faith in divine reality and its manifestation in our daily activities. There is a real state of sublime bliss that comes only after continuous and deep meditation of the sacred Name. Not through flights of fancy or magical tricks but only through one's meditation is this spiritual energy released.

As the Name is purity itself, human actions need to be exemplary to earn divine grace. This outcome is reached only through total submission of one's intents and purposes to higher aspirations of the soul and to an unquestioned acceptance of the divine reality.

Meditation 13

A believer gains wisdom,
consciousness, and awareness.
A believer gains inner
and outer mindfulness.

A believer does not go
stumbling and hobbling.
A believer is not terrorized
by death's calling.

Such is the power
of Your immaculate denomination,
that we know it
only through total submission.

Our faith in divine reality gives us numerous gifts: wisdom, consciousness, understanding, and mindfulness. Our mind is opened to extraordinary experiences. We overcome the fear of death, and we become conscious of the true potential of our soul. There are a multitude of gifts for us to possess and cherish. This meditation describes some of them.

Foremost is the gift of wisdom, the expression of our higher mind. Wisdom here has a different meaning than what is commonly understood. A wise person is said to be one who knows the ways of the world, or who is able to grasp technical or professional knowledge. That kind of wisdom is important and it is also a divine gift, but there is a higher wisdom based on truth, love, and right living. It is the wisdom that makes us aware of ultimate causes and effects. Where do we come from and where are we going? What are the various cycles of births and deaths that we have passed through? What forms of life have we already inhabited? What is the broad direction of our evolution? How could we hasten our movement toward our final destination? How are we to lead our life so that we become worthy of divine love?

The answers to these questions are not simple, but we have the option to follow the dictates of the Name and to place our trust in the divine will. We have to become divine instruments to spread love and compassion, remembering our Creator with every breath we take and keeping our body clean and healthy so that the abode of the soul is clean and healthy. This is the essence of divine wisdom, a wisdom that is a precondition of enlightenment.

Consciousness or awareness is another divine gift. Our consciousness is essential to our living. In fact, this is the only quality that separates those who are living from those who are dead. But the real gift here is the higher consciousness: a state of mind that enables us to distinguish the real from the unreal, the truth from the falsehood, the permanent from the transient, the spirit from the matter, the here and now from the eternal. Once we attain this level of consciousness, death ceases to be any threat to our being. We get to know the true identity of our soul-self that has always lived and will never cease to be.

A truly realized person has consciousness to fathom the inner reaches of self. Our inner awareness is a reflection of what is outside, the physical reality that can be seen with our eyes and touched by our hands. But once we attain the higher level of consciousness, the difference between what is inside and what is outside tends to disappear. We can see ourselves as the projection of a larger whole, active participants in the miracle of this divine creation. Our breath is the subtle connection between these two realities. The air that we breathe brings the promise of life. The air that we exhale is an act of meditation: an invisible salute to the divine mystery, a mixing of particles that were once part of ourselves with the universal flow of energy. This realization—that inner and outer realities exist as interdependent conditions, each enriching the other— is at the very heart of mindful living.

The test of our true belief is the stability of our mind and action. An unstable mind is a dangerous companion, meaninglessly meandering from one object to the other. Unstable actions are always halfhearted. We do things that do not appeal to us. We follow paths unaware of their final destinations. But once we come to accept the true reality of our being and the total sweep of the divine power, once we subdue our ego to the ultimate submission of self to the dictates of God, our mind becomes stable and peaceful and our actions become a model for others to follow.

A true believer has no fear of death or dying. Our physical death is only a new beginning, our chance to attain immortality, an opportunity to live in the presence of God. Our "death" in this life can bring us freedom from the pains of subsequent births and deaths. This is an opportunity, but can we really make this transition? Much depends on what we do in this life. If we have allowed the Name to become a part of our being, if we have put absolute trust in the will of God, if we have done good and have spoken well, our chances of entry into the divine realm are brightened. If our life is spent in the pursuit of worldly pleasures and goods, we will be unable to avoid the cycles of birth and death, with the attendant pain and suffering.

Meditation 14

A believer's path is unfettered
and self-directing.
A believer departs this world
with honor and lauding.

A believer does not stray
into ritualistic ceremonies.
A believer follows
the virtuous testimonies.

Such is the power
of Your immaculate denomination,

91

that we know it
only through total submission.

A believer's spiritual path is straightforward; there are no obstacles, no barriers. There is only one goal. Sideshows hold no attractions. There are no sights and sounds that distract attention. Such single-mindedness, such passionate pursuit of a single goal is the result of an inner urge, an inner flow of energy that keeps the believer moving in the same direction at all times. Every milestone is a step closer to God. There may be temporary setbacks, but a true believer's faith is never lost. And faith cannot be lost if divine acclaim is earned every step of the way. Meandering tracks, although deceptively attractive to look at, hold no fascination to this traveler. The sense of duty and the courage of one's convictions is so strong that total submission to the dictates of divine reality are not forgotten.

How is one to find the true path and follow it? The Guru's answer is to make an alliance with virtue. When we become virtuous, the path shows itself. There is no need to search for it because virtue is an anchor that does not allow us to go astray. As Macauliffe has interpreted one of the key lines in this meditation: "By obeying God, one proceeds in ecstasy on his path." And how does one obey God? By leading a virtuous life, which means having right thoughts and actions, a sense of humility, a willingness to share one's wealth and skills with others, and a heart filled with the love of God. These are some of the building blocks of a virtuous life and a practical way of obeying the will of God.

Meditation 15

A believer reaches the gates
of enlightenment and immortality.
A believer liberates loved ones
from life-death brutality.

A believer liberates self
and disciples seeking divine solace.
A believer, O Nanak, does not have
to wander for divine grace!

Such is the power
of Your immaculate denomination,
that we know it
only through total submission.

A true believer has no problem in attaining a soul life, a state that assures the greatest freedom of all, the freedom from being and nonbeing. Such is the blessed state of mind of the person who achieves enlightenment that it even impacts the lives of friends and relatives and others. They, too, can become divinely blessed through this act of association with a true believer.

This meditation assures us that the rewards for keeping one's faith are many and truly enriching. Not only are doors to eternal happiness and bliss opened, there is no dearth of material possessions either. These possessions may not hold much attraction to a person in search of the divine, but they can make a difference in determining the comfort level in which spiritual interests are pursued. Only a true believer can reap this harvest.

There are several related arguments in this meditation. First, if we have true faith, we shall find the path to liberation of our soul. Second, once we find these openings, we not only can cross into a new dimension of time and space, but can help our loved ones to do so too. Third, true faith liberates not only the disciple but also the preceptor, who is our guru or mentor. When the disciple takes one step forward closer to God, the preceptor also advances as a true liberator of souls. Last, but not least, when we strongly maintain our faith, we no longer wander in search of divine grace. It is bestowed on us every step of the way.

Meditation 16

They are blessed
whom You select.
They are honored
in Your court for their intellect.

They brighten the heavenly court
with their spiritual flame.
They find their minds dipped
in the meditation of Your name.

They try to describe You
after a good deal of reflection.
But Your doings are beyond
human enumeration.

Dharma's bull
is born of compassion,
and it holds the earth
in equalization.

This discovery enlightens
and makes us truthful.
How much load is carried
by the mythical bull?

But there are planets
and galaxies afar.
Who have carried
their loads so far?

There are different species
and colors they enshrine,
written by the ever-flowing pen
of the Divine.

Does anyone know how complete
the full account might be?
If an account is written,
how extensive might that be?

How powerful is the measure
of Your manifestation?
Who can estimate the greatness
of Your benediction?

You created the universe
with a single injunction,
and there emerged many a flowing river
and inundation.

What power do I have to describe You
and Your creation?

My powerlessness precludes
even a simple act of sacrifice!

Whatever pleases You
will public good secure.
Glory of the Formless One
shall forever endure.

Truly honored are those who are divinely selected. They understand the secrets of creation—of natural and physical phenomena like birds, flowering trees, and rivers. Ordinary human beings have no power to describe creation in this manner. Our power stems only from the Creator. If it does not come as a divine gift, it does not come at all

This meditation is exceptionally beautiful. It covers an immense range of themes. It talks about our moral and intellectual development, spiritual awakening, environmental ethics, and our relationship with the Creator and the creation.

Those who are chosen by God are morally and intellectually superior. They have their minds fixed on God. They do not think about anything else. Nothing else really matters to them.

The basis of the divine law is love and compassion, which we need to understand in dynamic terms. Love and compassion are the foundations of divine actions, but these are not static constructs. They are more like flows of positive energy, fountains or springs from which unending flows of mercy, affection, and acceptance continue uninterrupted for the benefit of all creation. All beings, therefore, are eligible for a second or a third chance. It is never too late for us to seek atonement. And whenever we come forward, our call is answered.

Once we understand and accept these simple truths, our mind is opened to the mysteries of creation mythology. Whether our planet stands on the horns of a mythical bull, or is part of a very complex array of solar systems and galaxies, we are sure to discover the truth. Who controls this huge universe? Whose command extends over these intergalactic distances that are difficult to measure and nearly impossible to explain. Did it all start with a "big bang," the singular explosion of energy at the beginning of the creation of this universe? Will it all end in a "big crunch," a massive contraction of all energy when this universe comes to an end? Who created black holes from which nothing, not even light, can escape? Can we ever discover these secrets?

The meditation shows us a path of discovery. This discovery is not separate from the discovery of God, because, in reality, the Creator and the creation are one. There are no secrets that are hidden from the sight of a true believer. It is the power of our faith that opens all these doors to mystical realms hidden from our eyes.

The meditation celebrates biodiversity. There are so many creatures on this planet that their number is beyond any intelligent guess. Even the best research scientists have no answer to the question of how much exists now, how much has already become extinct, and how much is in the process of evolving into other forms. Is this all happening by chance, as the unfolding of a Darwinian horror story? The question is also an answer to resolving the mystery. Nothing happens by chance. Science can explain some parts but others it has to leave to speculation.

The current debate on the preservation of biodiversity misses one essential point. Biodiversity needs to be preserved, not only for its medicinal, recreational, educational, and scientific values (all these goals are important by themselves), but because we have no right to destroy this divine creation. It is only God who has the absolute power to destroy something or to keep it alive. Human interference in these matters is a violation of the divine law.

The unconditional acceptance of the divine will is a first step toward our own self-awareness and spiritual awakening. Nature can be a great teacher and healer in our spiritual quest. Creation is not separate from the Creator, in the same way as any work of art is inseparable from the artist. But this is a limiting analogy. It is not just a work of art, confined to a small space in an art gallery. We are talking about an act of creation whose boundaries over space and time are unfathomable. This complexity is irreducible to any simple hypothesis. We can use science or logic to unfold this, but there is no better tool than the practice of meditation. Once we experience self-awakening and allow the divine flow of energy to radiate to the darkest reaches of our soul, the mysteries of creation will slowly unfold.

Meditation 17

Countless are meditations
and countless are ways of devotion.
Countless are worships
and countless are ways of renunciation.

Countless are scriptures
and countless those who are spiritual seekers.
Countless are yogis
who are indifferent to worldly encounters.

Countless are devotees
who ponder on things veritable.
Countless are the pious
and countless are those who are charitable.

Countless are warriors
who face the wrath of their opposition.
Countless are worshipers
who believe in silent contemplation.

What power do I have to describe You
and Your creation?

My powerlessness precludes
even a simple act of sacrifice!

Whatever pleases You
will public good secure.
Glory of the Formless One
shall forever endure.

There are different ways of worship. Differences among men and women are reflected in the ways they connect with God. There are those of us who are satisfied with saying our prayers in a simple manner. But some are not content with this. They think that their prayer is incomplete without inflicting physical suffering on themselves. This suffering can take several forms: fasting for a number of days at a time; sitting in a certain body posture for long periods of time; inflicting pain through various other means, including sleeping on hard floors. There are those who read the holy scriptures and meditate to satisfy their spiritual quest. And there are others who needlessly inflict pain on themselves, thinking that God would be pleased to see them suffer. These are all misperceptions. How could the source of greatest love and compassion ever wish to inflict pain on us?

There is no need to go through rituals involving pain and discomfort. Nothing matters except the purity of one's prayer. When the Name comes to our lips from the inner reaches of our soul, that, itself, becomes the best form of prayer.

A distinction is made here between two forms of worship, one based on knowledge and the other on love. We can use our intellect to reflect on the nature of God. We can ask questions, and answer them with all the power of our intellect. This is what philosophers are trained to do. They can handle abstractions, using their mental models to conceptualize what is known and what is unknown. This is a form of worship but perhaps it is not suited to everyone's needs.

The other mode of worship is relatively simple: it is based on love. In this mode, there is no need to ask questions. In fact, there are no questions. When one's heart is filled with love and compassion, there is nothing more to be known. There is no place for any doubt; there is no room for any skepticism. The path of love is the most direct and the most accessible path to enlightenment. God is love as well as truth. When we love God without any qualifiers, in return we get pure and unalloyed love that is true and eternal.

The worship of God is the fundamental right of all beings, human as well as other species. It has nothing to do with the state of evolution of one's body or mind. Birds sing and animals howl as their way of celebrating the glory of this creation. Human beings certainly are more complex. They express their devotion in different ways. Sometimes the rich and powerful feel that they have a greater right to display their faith than those who are poor. These are misconceptions. In our relationship with God, all of us stand on the same footing. Our stature might differ in accord with our spiritual evolution, but material things have no significance. It is true that rich people can travel more easily to holy lands than poor people, but that begs the question: is there a place on earth which is not holy? When we close our eyes and feel the presence of God, we sanctify the ground on which we stand. This experience does not cost any money; it needs only our readiness to embrace our Creator. When we are ready, God shows us the way.

Meditation 18

Countless are fools
who are appallingly ignorant.
Countless are thieves
who are disgustingly repugnant.

Countless are rulers
who tyrannize.
Countless are tyrants
who terrorize.

Countless are sinners
who have sin in their blood.
Countless are liars
who wander in falsehood.

Countless are wretches
who have impure minds and live in filthy bins.
Countless are slanderers
who will carry the burden of their sins.

Nanak humbly expresses this thought:
My powerlessness precludes
even a simple act of sacrifice!

Whatever pleases You
will public good secure.
Glory of the Formless One
shall forever endure.

There are people who lead lowly forms of life. They are unaware that this life has been gifted to them after a long evolutionary struggle. This is the time when they can get closer to God, but because they are spiritually deficient they do not know the opportunities they are missing. We do not need a degree in divinity for God realization. We need a wisdom that is the wisdom of the heart: knowing that the love of God is available to us when we want it.

There are people who steal and rob. They take away what does not belong to them from their innocent victims. They think that they can get away with stealing. They are ignorant because they do not see the reach of the divine law. No unworthy action goes unpunished, in the same way that no good action goes unrewarded. There may be a delay in divine justice but there is no avoiding it.

There are autocratic leaders or tyrants who oppress their own people and deny them basic human rights. Political oppression does not last forever, however. It can cast a long shadow and dishearten many, but not those who have faith in God's mercy and a belief in the final victory of good over evil. No tyrant lives forever. There is a moment of truth for every tyrant who thought he could trample the world under his feet. Flames of love and hope that burn in the heart of a true believer can suddenly explode into the light of many suns when the merciful hand of God ends the reign of tyranny. Tyrants finally get a taste of their own medicine. They can lose their dignity and life at the hands of those whom they once oppressed.

When one leads a sinful life or engages in lies or talks ill of people who are God-fearing, these are actions that take us away from God. Once we go in the wrong direction on the path of ignorance, there is no hope for our redemption. We have to head in the right direction to find our own sacred space. The map we need for this purpose is the map of a loving heart. Then we shall never be lost because our path will always shine.

Meditation 19

Countless are Your names
and countless Your abodes.
Beyond reach are Your countless worlds
and celestial modes.

To call these simply countless
is a limiting description.
Through words, we chant Your name
and show our devotion.

Through words, we get knowledge
and learn to sing Your praises.
Through words, is recorded
our destiny and its mazes.

Yet these written words are not binding
on the Supreme Deity.
What You decree, we receive
as Your gift to humanity.

All creation is Your manifestation
and without You there is no habitation.
What power do I have to describe You
and Your creation?

My powerlessness precludes
even a simple act of sacrifice!

Whatever pleases You
will public good secure.
Glory of the Formless One
shall forever endure.

This meditation provides a glimpse of the divine kingdom. It is only a glimpse because the true glory of God is beyond words; it is revealed only to those who have earned the right to experience this sublime vision.

Unlike human beings, who might have one or two names and dwellings, God has millions of names and abodes. Being in one place does not mean that the Supreme cannot be in other places. There is no place in this whole universe that is free of divine presence.

God may be seen in various forms. These manifestations are without any limit. The blossoming of a flower, the flight of an eagle, the beauty of a lake, the roar of oceanic waves, and the notes of music floating in the air on a dark night— these are some of the manifestations of God's presence. Once we open our heart to the mysteries of this divine creation, we can gain access to God's limitless manifestations. Because we are constrained in terms of our reach and modes of expression, we pour out our love for the Divine through prayer and meditation. We have to depend on these modalities because we know of no other way of expressing ourselves. But once we are fully engrossed in our prayer, words are no longer words. Everything turns into a soul transforming experience.

Meditation 20

When hands, feet, and body
are covered with slime,
water washes, cleans,
and purifies before time.

When clothes are soiled
and foul smell they emit,
a cake of soap clears the filth
and makes them fit.

When our soul is overlaid
with sin and shame,

it will be cleansed only
by the love of Your name.

Saints and sinners are not made
by being so-called.
Good and bad actions are known
and our future is destined.

As we sow,
so shall we eat.
With divine will, O Nanak,
this journey do we repeat!

Our soul is a vehicle for realization of God. But our body is spatially constrained; our hands reach out only for a few feet. However, there is a part of us that is unbounded. We call it "mind"—the center of our consciousness. And at the deepest level, there is the center of our cosmic consciousness that we call our "soul." We know relatively little about our mind and even less about our soul. Scientists are exploring the extended power of the mind. Several studies about the power of prayer have shown that, through what is called "intercessory prayer," we can heal people who are miles away from us. This could not be possible unless our mind is part of an energy field that exerts influence over long distances. Our mind is not confined to our skull, like our brain; it is an extended substance whose true power we have yet to realize.

Whatever is known about soul is the subject of great controversy. Does soul exist? If so, where is it located? One simple way to describe soul is to call it the "essence" of our being that remains after our body is reduced to dust. It is the essence that continues to move on its journey of "soul making." Our soul and not our body meets with God, if and when we make this transition. God knows our essence; our earthly body that we leave behind has little significance. That is why this meditation highlights the importance of our soul and how we should nourish it in this life.

When our body is unclean, we can easily wash it with soap and fragrant liquids. When our clothes get dirty, they can be easily laundered. But when our soul is steeped in sin, when we have reached a level of sinfulness that has even soiled our soul it cannot be washed by any earthly substance. No soap can clean it. The only thing that can help us is prayer and meditation. We can always ask for forgiveness for our actions, but to gain this realization, we need a period of meditation and recitation of the Name.

Along with this strict regimen of prayer and meditation, we have to watch our actions. What are we really doing? Are we causing pain or suffering to others or are we bringing happiness and joy?

According to the Law of Karma, every action has a reaction. The seeds of our actions will gradually fertilize; whether they are for our good or bad will depend on the nature of our actions. Our good deeds enrich and nourish our soul, our harmful actions impoverish our soul. We can degrade ourselves to a level where we can brutalize or kill children without any sense of remorse, as is seen in many parts of the world today. On the other hand, a life of love and self-sacrifice, of devotion and compassion is uplifting. It raises our physical and moral stature. And more than anything else, it enhances the reach of our soul. Beyond the dazzling glare of the tunnel of light is the permanent abode of our soul. Are we foolishly going to miss this chance of reaching our goal?

Meditation 21

Pilgrimage, atonement,
compassion, and creed
will fetch us merit, if any,
tiny as a sesame seed.

By hearing, obeying,
and loving Your name divine,

we purify ourselves
and bathe in the sacred inner shrine.

All virtue resides in You
and none in me that others can see.
Without virtuous actions,
no one is a true devotee.

My salutation to You,
O Creator of Maya and the sacred word!
Truth and beauty ever reside
in Your blissful heart and word.

What was the occasion, what hour,
what date, and day of the week?
What was the season,
what month did the Creator seek?

Pundit knows not the time,
as it is not mentioned in the Puran.
Kazi knows not the time
after reading the Koran.

Yogi knows not the day, season,
or month of this calendar.
Only the Creator knows the intricacies
of this cosmic grammar.

How should I address, describe,
and know Thee, O love of mine?
O Nanak, we offer discourses
but are unable to properly define!

There is only one Supreme Creator,
who is our sole mover.
O Nanak, the pretentious will not have
much glory to uncover!

There is sublime beauty and deep meaning to be found in this
meditation. It gives us the secret of true self-realization. It is
not through any rituals that we realize God; it is not by making trips to holy lands; it is not through any number of out-

ward actions that we get closer to God. All these actions, although good in practice, bring very little reward. Total inner transformation is required. We have to love the Supreme Being with all our sincerity and goodness. We have to place everything at God's command, holding back nothing. Only then can we begin our spiritual journey—a journey of a billion cosmic miles that begins with a simple resolve.

In the second part of this meditation, the Guru comes back to God's grandeur and the mystery of creation. We enjoy talking about special moments in our lives: the time of our graduation, the day of our marriage, the time when we became a parent. These events are special, but what about the event of creation itself? Can we compare what happens in the life of the universe with what happens in our lives? There is obviously no comparison. However, it is humbling to remember how small our most joyous moments are, compared to the biggest event of all—the creation of this universe itself.

Many people lay claim to this knowledge. They think that they know the secret. They are wrong. No one person knows it all. Nor is it written in any book. The secret of creation resides solely in the mind of the Creator. No one else has any clue, but there are many good guesses. If we wish to share this secret, we have to aim at reaching a collective "spiritual" consciousness in order to witness the wondrous powers of this Creator.

Meditation 22

> Millions are the lower regions
> and countless spaces of unbounded vastness.
> Wise ones have searched in vain,
> and the Vedas, too, declare helplessness.
>
> Semitic texts count eighteen thousand,
> although there is only one essence.

Your infinity no one can measure;
this search is of little consequence.

Only the Divine, O Nanak,
knows the True Self!

There are no visible limits to this universe. There are no boundaries of any kind. As we go farther into outer space, we discover more and more. No end seems to exist. But the Creator, who created this universe, knows the answer—how it began and how it will end. All other answers are guesses. The work of the Creator can't be subjected to any human measurement. Our capacity to assess this phenomenon is totally inadequate.

God has innumerable abodes. A literal translation of the opening line of this meditation would mean a hundred thousand worlds below and countless heavens above! This is a limiting interpretation. As revealed by modern astrological sciences, the number of solar systems, galaxies, and stars is nearly limitless, beyond human calculation. This is precisely the point this meditation wishes to convey. The count is futile because we can spend several lifetimes doing this calculation and, yet, our count will not be complete. The "wise" among us (should we call them "scientists"?) can make claims but their knowledge is incomplete. Many holy scriptures attempt to explain this universe (some make wildly inaccurate guesses), but only God knows the correct answer. We are reminded of Greek philosopher Empedocles' observation: "The nature of God is a circle, of which the center is everywhere and the circumference is nowhere."

In this meditation, the Guru explains a central tenet of his cosmological belief: the boundarylessness of this created universe. It is limitless from the human perspective, but not from that of the Creator's. God alone knows the answer. All of our guesses are wild and meaningless; they are just "not this, not this" (na iti, na iti) type. Instead of making guesses, we

108

could better spend our time putting our faith in the Glorious One, who knows it all.

Meditation 23

Devotees who worship You
know not Your greatness,
as rivers and rivulets know not
the oceanic vastness.

Kings with wealth greater than
the sweep of an ocean
are worthless if their minds are not
filled with Your devotion.

Spiritual life involves making hard choices. We reach the place where we set out to go. But are we making the right decision? A river headed in the direction of the ocean does not worry about its destination. It knows intuitively that it will reach its rightful destination. The choices we make have consequences, whether we realize it or not.

There is no way for us to know the full sweep of divine power through the simple acts of prayer and meditation, particularly in the initial stages of our spiritual life. Is this an opportunity, or is this a constraint? This meditation gives us optimism. It is human nature to want to be rewarded every step of the way. If we don't achieve results in a short time, we are likely to get disheartened.

We need to remember that divine love is its own reward. The river knows that eventually it will flow into the ocean. The thought of not reaching the ocean does not bother it. The same process holds true for a true follower. Once we are on the correct path, we will get there. That is the promise. Our true worth is our spiritual strength and the intensity of our devotion to the Name. A vast amount of wealth or worldly power means nothing if our heart is not filled with the love of God. A skeptic's true worth is smaller than the tiniest creature.

Another interpretation of this meditation is that, even with all the devotion, God's true greatness would not be fully revealed to us. But should it matter? When the river enters the ocean, its contents are no longer those of the river. The river's contents already have become part of the ocean. Its water doesn't ask the question, "What is the nature of water in this vast ocean?" It is the ocean.

Meditation 24

Infinite is the measure of divine attributes
and their numbering.
Infinite is the measure of divine actions
and divine giving.

Infinite is the measure of divine perception
and divine listening.
Infinite is the measure of divine mind
and divine thinking.

Infinite is the measure of divine shaping
and divine creating.
Infinite is the dimension of its beginning
and ending.

Many have yearned to know the limits
of divine creation.
Yet this search ended in vain,
without a clue or information.

This limit no one really knows;
the more we say, the greater it shows.

You are the Supreme Being
and Your seat is highest in fame.
Highly praised and exalted
is Your loving name.

If there was someone, just any one,
with Your prime stature,
only then would we know
the meaning of Your vesture.

You are the sole judge and evaluator
of Your greatness.
O Nanak, treasure the gift of God's mercy
and graciousness!

If there is one word to describe God's unrestrained power, it would be "infinite"—meaning boundless, limitless, unbounded, inexhaustible, incalculable, and measureless. Infinite is a measure that has no specific count. It is true of God's creation (there are no limits), God's ability to see and hear everything (nothing is hidden), and God's ability to bless and redeem all beings (it is never too late to ask for God's mercy). Many people have attempted to know these cosmic boundaries, but their efforts ended in failure. If anyone had the ability to accomplish this task, that person would have the same stature as God. Yet this is impossible. For the most part, human beings have problems dealing with the concept of "infinite" because it means dark and empty spaces without any definite boundaries.

In order for us to deal with the infinite, we have to do what the poet and philosopher, William Blake, suggested: "If the doors of perception were cleansed, everything would appear to man as it is, infinite." The process of cleansing the doors of perception is a spiritual process. This is another way of saying that the infinite cannot be defined with our ordinary experience, nor does it have to be. If God's greatness is infinite, there will be no end to our description. The meditation expresses this paradox in a beautiful line: "The more we say, the greater it shows." Think of a story that expands by the very act of its telling!

Meditation 25

Your generosity
we cannot in word record.
The Beloved seeks
not a seed we can afford.

Even the mighty seek
Your favor and endearment.
And others, whose numbers
are beyond good judgment.
There are those
who rot in evil encampment.

There are those
who receive without gratitude.
And others,
who consume with servitude.

There are those
who are victims of hunger and chastisement.
But they accept this
as a divine gift of spiritual fulfillment.

Your benevolence
can break our mortal bond.
No one can interfere
with the divine plan, here or beyond.

If any fool ventures
to unfold Your mystery,
unlimited blows will that person receive
for such buffoonery.

You know our needs
and give to us carefully.
Only a few acknowledge this
and live gracefully.

If You be so pleased
to confer Your blessings,

the recipient, O Nanak,
will be the King of Kings!

God is generous in giving and does not expect anything in return. But this does not mean that we should fail to acknowledge what we receive. We should give our thanks in whatever way possible. But the worst sin of all is the lack of a simple acknowledgment. When we are imprisoned by our ego, we are more likely to say, "Yes, I did it" when we should say, "With divine grace, it has become possible for me to achieve what I have achieved in this life." Such an acknowledgment is the first step on the road to our spirituality.

This meditation is a true celebration of divine generosity and benevolence. Such is the scope and measure of giving that it is difficult to describe it in words. God gives generously without expecting anything in return. The seekers are not only the poor and needy but also the mighty and powerful. All of us need divine generosity, irrespective of our status in life. Most of us acknowledge these gifts with humility and remembrance, but there are those who are ungrateful, and their behavior shows it. They make their accomplishments look like their personal achievements, as if there was no divine facilitation of the factors that led to their success. Nothing is achieved in life without divine grace.

Arrogance is a fallacy in which the foolish indulge. They forget that divine intervention is needed, not only for material things but also to break the bonds of mortality—the endless cycles of birth and death. Arrogant people are here for a prolonged period of suffering, because they are unworthy of God's most generous reward—the gift of immortality.

Meditation 26

Priceless are Your qualities
and measures.

Priceless are Your trades
and treasures.

Priceless are what You provide
and what is taken away.
Priceless are those who are absorbed
in Your love every day.

Priceless are Your law
and the court of corrections.
Priceless are the scales
and weights that measure actions.

Priceless are Your blessings,
marks, and benedictions.
Priceless are Your benevolence
and proclamations.

Priceless, priceless beyond words,
is all that defies expression.
Those who repeat Your name
are immersed in deep devotion.

Vedas and Puranas attempt to explain
Your greatness.
Scholars read this
and proffer their thoughtfulness.

Brahma and Indra attempt
to laud You.
Gopis and Govinda attempt
to praise You.

Shiva and ascetics sing
of You.
Many enlightened souls
acclaim You.

Demons and demigods
revere You.
Demigods and silent meditators
worship You.

Many have said
and more will attempt to say.
Many have spoken
before making their headway.

If You were to create
as many people as already exist,
they will fail to portray
Your greatness, even if we insist.

You are as exalted
as You wish to appear in your fullness.
O Nanak, the True One guards the secret
of Its own greatness!
Someone attempting to describe You
will manifest foolishness.

Pricelessness of the divine "trade" is hard to describe. In the realm of the spirit, worldly measures are of little use. Metaphorically speaking, traders who come in search of godly gifts have access to an unlimited range of precious things, meaning mystical experiences of the highest order. The store of divine love can never be emptied. Devotees have the whole treasure at their disposal.

The central currency of this trade is love—unconditional love. We love God without any expectation, and our love is returned to us in more ways than we can count. The sanctity of the divine court is matched only by the paths of righteousness that intersect this sacred space. There is a precise measurement of our actions; even an ounce of good would weigh a ton.

Such is the beauty and grandeur of the divine court that all scriptures contain long descriptions of its mystical delights. Sages and holy incarnations, such as Brahma, Indra, Krishna and his companions, Buddhas of supreme enlightenment, ascetics, and demons, have all sung praises of the One who is the only True Being of this universe. This pro-

cession of sages, singing hymns of praise, has come and gone
but one reality has not changed. Only God is uncreated;
only God is immortal. All greatness, all goodness, stems from
this singular source. If we know this source, we are enlightened and truly empowered. Although not pretending to
describe the unknown shows true wisdom, only the foolish
actually would attempt to do so.

Meditation 27

Where is the gate,
where is the great mansion?
Where is the place for You
to watch Your creation?

Countless are the instruments
that make divine melodies.
Countless are the songs,
and many are the players of symphonies.

Wind, water, and fire sing praises,
while Dharmaraj keeps appreciating.
Shiva, Brahma, and goddesses laud Thee
with sheer beauty permeating.

Chitra and Gupta keep record,
while Dharmaraj does the adjudicating.
God Indra sings with other godlings,
who also find it truly exciting.

Saints in deep trance chant the Divine Name
in soul nourishing contemplation.
The self-restrained, virtuous, and contented
join in this jubilation.

Scholars and sages laud You
in texts written in many ages.
Mermaids extol You
from upper, lower, and middle stages.

Fourteen sacred objects sing
with sixty-eight sacred places.
Mighty heroes and four sources of life
pay their homages.

There are those who sing
as a sign of their thanksgiving.
There are others, O Nanak,
who are beyond imagining.

You are True and
Supreme Truth is Thy manifestation.
You are and shall remain
the sole Creator of this creation.

Choosing different species and colors,
You made this sensual reality.
Beholding this creation,
You provide testimony to Your immensity.

Your actions are Your pleasure,
restrained by no other demand.
You are, O Nanak, the Supreme Ruler
who is fully in command!

The City of God is the most beautiful of all places. It is the brightest and the purest of all places. It is the center of all spiritual and creative energy of our universe. We may not be able to experience the sanctity of this place, but we can picture in our mind the exquisite arrangement of various natural elements and the presence of gods and goddesses, who are all subordinate to divine will. It is a place of perfect harmony, the creation at its very best. If the thought of this sacred place is so uplifting, can we imagine what an experience it would offer to any one who actually goes there!

This is a vivid and deeply moving description of the holy realm. We want to know where our Beloved lives. Where is the gate and where is the boundary wall? All the sense of divine wonder and excitement is captured in this one question. Only if we are divinely inspired, can our imagination succeed in visualizing something as majestic and mysterious.

The place is wrapped in sounds made by all kinds of musical instruments. There are singers and minstrels singing songs of love in ragas of unparalleled perfection. Even nature joins this musical chorus, with wind, water, and fire providing the background rhythms and sounds.

Those present in this divine court have prescribed roles. The recording angels, Chitra and Gupta, keep track of good and bad actions of every being. The presence of other deities, such as Shiva and Brahma, is marked. Indra is seated on his throne. In addition to these deities, there are warriors, scholars, and heroes. There are sacred sights and places, the best and the most beautiful pieces of this magnificent creation, that enhance the magical quality of the divine residence. The Creator, having created this universe, beholds the creation as an expression of the most perfect love for all created beings and objects.

Meditation 28

Take earrings of contentment, and carry
the begging-bowl of honest effort.
Let ashes of awareness embrace your body
as a sign of spiritual support.

Make the awareness of approaching mortality
your patched garment;
let purity be a way of life,
with the staff of faith acting as a deterrent.

Stay closer to like-minded associates
who are from the same upper world.

When you conquer the mind,
you conquer the world.

Let me hail Thee, O Supreme Being!
Without the beginning or the end,
living through all time.

Being a traveler on the spiritual path requires us to change our way of life. We should seek total contentment. We should be modest about ourselves and make a sincere effort to channel our energies to meet our desired ends. Meditation should become an essential part of our living. We should conquer the fear of death by being aware of its imminence. We should spend most of our time with the same spiritual brotherhood to which we belong. This should help us in gaining greater control of our mental faculties. It is only through controlling our mind that we can make progress. Conquering our mind (ego-mind) is metaphorically equivalent to conquering the world.

Once we truly believe in God, we attain internal contentment, outward modesty, soulful living, freedom from fear of death, and hope for atonement. Any human being searching for fulfillment must have a contented mind. Contentment must be a visible part of our life, like an ornament that is worn for the pleasure of being seen. Being modest about ourselves and our accomplishments is the quality of a true achiever. Our modesty should match that of the beggar who walks around with a begging bowl.

We should be so absorbed in the meditation of the Name that our prayer wraps around our body like a coating of ash. We need to lead a life that is free from the fear of death. We should be unspoiled like a virgin's body, doing what is right rather than what is convenient. Our greatest strength is the staff symbolizing our faith in God. Faith is our true strength. Nothing more is needed.

Seekers of the spirit should be careful about the teachers and spiritual associates whom they select. They should keep the company of truly realized persons, people who can be their guides on the spiritual path. The meditation tells us a simple secret of living: if we conquer our mind, we shall conquer the world. What is simple for a spiritually developed person is not simple for most of us. Instead of conquering our ego-mind, we like to lead our life as its prisoner. This can change if we persist in doing the right thing, following our path with passion and courage.

Meditation 29

Let divine knowledge be our nourishment,
compassion our treasure.
Let us listen to the internal melody
to experience true rapture.

You are the real owner
of this vast universe.
Wealth and rituals are diversions,
and even perverse.

Union and separation are
for Deity to arrange.
We receive what our good actions
get in exchange.

Let me hail Thee, O Supreme Being!
Without the beginning or the end,
living through all time.

The most challenging task for us is to take care of our inner self. That is the storehouse of divine knowledge. We may call it "soul." Nothing except our soul is going to go beyond to experience the beauteous vision of God. What do we need as we go? Divine knowledge provides nourishment, compassion governs our dealings with the world, and divine music, which beats in every human heart reminds us of God's presence.

The search for God is most rewarding at the start, during the entire course of the journey, and on reaching the goal. Divine knowledge provides nourishment for our inner self. We know how to nourish our body, but nourishment and enrichment of the inner self is not easily understood. What do we need to carry with us on this journey? Compassion is the first requirement. A compassionate heart alone can show us the path. We need to walk while listening to the divine melody that beats in our heart.

We need to exercise caution so that we follow the true path. There are many paths that promise short-term rewards or material gains through magical and miraculous acts. Those are the false ways. There is no magic on the true path, except the magic of the divine glow that surrounds and protects all incoming souls; there are no miracles, except the miracle of love that is perhaps the biggest miracle of all.

We need to remember how everything is divinely ordained. The pleasure of the union and the pain of separation are rewards or punishments for our actions. If we reap a bountiful harvest because of our good actions, then God is our protector without our ever knowing about it.

Meditation 30

The Primal Mother, through a mysterious union,
delivered three sons, known as the holy trinity.
One was the creator, second was the preserver,
and the third was the judge of human frivolity.

In reality, nothing happens without Your will,
O Savior Magnanimous.

Unseen to the trinity, You watch them all,
which is simply marvelous.

Let me hail Thee, O Primal Being!
Without the beginning or the end,
living through all time.

There is a mythological belief about different roles of gods who are given the responsibility of creating, nourishing, and destroying the universe (thereby making it ready for re-creation). Should such gods exist, they would have this power as the sons of the Supreme Creator, herein called the "Primal Mother." There is no power to create or destroy that is not drawn from the primal source we worship as God.

The Eternal Being made a dramatic plan involving creation of the world, its preservation, destruction and re-creation. The three sons of the Primal Mother, who are worshipped as gods in their own right, were made responsible for creating the universe (the work of Brahma), preserving and nourishing it (the role of Vishnu), and finally destroying it for re-creation (the task of Shiva). In reality, however, it is the will of the Supreme that is being expressed by these deities. Nothing is hidden from God who sees them, like everything else. There is only one source of all mystical power. The relationship of the Supreme to other gods and goddesses is like that of a principal to its agents. Agents have power as long as it is exercised in accordance with the wishes of the principal!

Meditation 31

Your throne and treasures
are in numerous worlds that hold all.
These places were fully
and adequately stocked once and for all.

The Creator, having created the universe,
watches over it.

122

O Nanak, the maker of Truth,
is Truth explicit.

Let me hail Thee, O Primal Being!
Without the beginning or the end,
living through all time.

Divine presence knows no limits, no boundaries. All the worlds have been fully provided for and are under constant vigil. Neither good nor evil has any place to hide. We can feel the divine presence, yet, in many respects, it seems that we are too far away in view of our own imperfections.

God's homes are located in all the worlds. Divine presence is limitless. No one can escape it. The founding principle of this empire of the spirit is compassion and equity. All human beings are given a reserve of divine mercy to draw upon like a bank account. No one gets more or less. We all start with the same balance, yet, in the end, some multiply their savings while others end up with negative balances. We may not see this organizing principle, but it operates at all times.

When bad things happen, we ask "Why me," or "Why now." Such reactions show our immaturity and lack of understanding of the laws of creation. There are no chance happenings; everything is part of the creative design. We should wait for those rare moments of illumination when miracles happen. These flashes of sudden enlightenment can be attributed to the fact that we are watched by God at all times and thus are exposed to the flow of divine energy. We are never away from divine guidance, especially when the True One has something to say to us: a reminder, a piece of advice. When we hear this inner voice, we need to stop, listen, and learn.

Meditation 32

If I had not one but one hundred thousand tongues
multiplying twentyfold as a simple matter.
A hundred thousand times
would I say Your name with all my power.

Such single-minded devotion
is a ladder that joins me with the Supreme Beloved.
The sound of the celestial song
raises even the lesser worm-like quadruped.

Only divine grace takes us there, O Nanak,
and let false ones boast and be evil-minded!

Prayer is the most effective way of making progress on the spiritual route. It brightens our entire being and gives us concentration that we can't get on the ordinary course. Prayer is not, as is commonly understood, a dry, endless repetition of a word or collection of words. Words are of least importance in a prayer. Our soul can express itself without words or in "soul expressions" that can't be translated into words. It is like a particle of light that pierces the darkness of our inner self, giving our body and the soul a purity we generally associate with angels.

Prayer may be used for various purposes: to ask for something for ourselves, to ask for something for those whom we love, to make a confession of wrongdoing, or simply to say the praise of the Beloved. Whatever the purpose, every prayer, in the end, is an effort to connect with the Universal Mind, the sublime source of all energy in this universe.

Even if we had a thousand tongues, the only proper use for them would be to say a prayer. Such is the magical healing quality of words that even the lowest creatures find comfort after hearing the sacred Name. In recent years, many experiments have been conducted to test the power of prayer.

124

In several cases, the results can't be explained rationally. The problem is our ignorance about our own inner power, which is a divine gift. In the words of the fifth century theologian, St. Augustine: "Seek not abroad, turn back into thyself, for in the inner man dwells the truth." And this truth finds its expression in the form of a prayer.

Meditation 33

I have no power to speak
or keep silent.
I have no power to ask
or be benevolent.

I have no power to live
or die of my own will or action.
I have no power to gain wealth
that causes mental commotion.

I have no power to gain consciousness
or divine knowledge, or to meditate.
I have no power to leave this world
or just to reincarnate.

One who has the power,
will use it as our caretaker.
By our own strength, O Nanak,
no one is a maker or a breaker!

This meditation summarizes our limitations as human beings. There are many things we don't control or can't do. But there is one thing we can easily do. We can choose God. By aligning ourselves with the Supreme Being, we break the bonds of our helplessness. We can really free ourselves to take part in the magic of life.

Without divine grace and compassion, we are completely helpless. We do not control our speech because that depends on the breath of life infused in us by the Divine Spirit. Some people are born speechless, some lose the power to speak because of illness. Ultimately, it depends on whether we are given the gift of life, a life that is complete in all respects. The power to move, to think, to speak, and to seek divine grace is all part of our enlightenment.

Meditation 34

You made nights,
seasons, lunar days and weekdays.
Air, water, fire,
and infernal walkways.

Installed in the middle is this earth
as a habitat for moral living.
Therein, You created beings
of all colors and shading.

Although they have different names
and infinite identities,
they are judged finally
by their moral proclivities.

You are Supreme Truth,
and true is Your transaction.
You accept and honor those
who really deserve redemption.

Their actions have earned them
a mark of recognition.
The imperfect are separated from the perfect
at this destination.
O Nanak, on reaching there,
we shall know about our selection!

Meditations 34 through 37 provide descriptions of five realms that are stages of our spiritual growth. The journey from "here" (our daily existence) to "there" (the state of self-realization) will be a long and arduous journey. Not all of us are capable of going the entire way. What happens when we travel one-third or one-half of the way? It is definitely better than not moving at all. Also, this is a journey that might take several lifetimes to complete. In the first stage, called the "moral realm" (*dharam khand*), the meditation emphasizes the need for moral living.

The Creator's art of creation is unparalleled in its perfection, beauty, and complexity. It includes the making of nights, seasons, lunar days, weekdays, wind, water, fire, and lower regions. In the midst of the higher and lower regions is our planet, Mother Earth, which is our abode and a place for us to grow and flourish during our stay here.

Earth is also a place for spiritual and moral living, where we can make ourselves worthy of divine forgiveness and grace. This does not mean following the dictates of an institutionalized religion. The spiritual path this meditation recommends is the belief in God and the need to abide by the principles that are at the core of several wisdom traditions.

With all its diversity, this earth is best suited for meditation of the sacred name. We have clean air and fresh water. Birds and animals are here to keep our company and provide a backdrop for our meditation.

In this realm, as in others, God is the Supreme Judge. Good deeds are rewarded. After the judgment is made, God treats us with compassion and forgiveness. Those who pass the test bear the mark of divine acceptance. Others, who fail to show the beauty of their spirit, are assigned tasks in the cycles of life and death. The minimum expectation is to abide by the principles, such as nonviolence, compassion, forgiveness, and charitable giving.

There are two operative principles of this realm: either our actions stand the test of moral scrutiny or we rely on God's grace and forgiveness. The entry into higher realms is based on more demanding spiritual standards, which only some of us are capable of fulfilling.

Meditation 35

The moral realm is the realm of moral deeds,
actions, and living.
Thereafter, follows the realm of knowledge,
which is quite amazing.

There are primal elements keeping company
with gods of extreme sacredness.
There are divine craftsmen crafting the universe
with different shades of loveliness.

There are fields of righteous action,
meditations of Dhruv on Meru Mountain.
There are abodes of Indra,
moons, suns, and the entire solar domain.

There are abodes of sages, seers,
and goddesses of utmost devotion.
There are demons, demigods,
and jewels churned out of oceanic commotion.

There are sources of creation,
forms of speech, and people of royal connection.
Countless, O Nanak, are the enlightened ones,
and there is no count of their reflection!

As we move to the realm of divine knowledge and wisdom *(jnan khand)*, we are given access to secrets of the creation of this universe. But in order to become eligible for this privileged information, we should have shown relentless pursuit in our life of mystical and spiritual knowledge. This is the realm of great gods and goddesses who perform tasks that are divinely assigned. Air, water, and fire are in various stages of making. To be in this realm is like being present on the day of creation. We can watch miracles that no human being has ever seen.

Meditations in this realm are of such pristine purity that only gods can practice them. Being there gives us an opportunity to learn true meditation at the feet of sages, such as Dhruv, who meditate on the most sacred mountain of all, Mount Meru. And there are places that are worthy of seats of meditation and enlightenment of gods.

Meditation 36

In the realm of divine knowledge,
there is an explosion of spiritual enlightenment.
There are mystic melodies
filling one's heart with joy and discernment.

In the realm of spiritual beauty,
there is an unfoldment of incomparable forms.
Many splendid shapes are crafted here,
which defy the usual norms.

The dramatic events in this realm,
if described, will look awkward.
Anyone who tries to say
will repent afterward.

Over here, soul consciousness, intellect, and emotions
are finely blended.
Miraculous powers of great seers
are divinely extended.

This meditation gives us a glimpse of the realm of spiritual beauty, the realm of spiritual enrichment and unfoldment *(saram khand)*. When our spirit unfolds, it is able to see such beauty, which was denied before. This is the realm where our spirit is crafted afresh as a consequence of our spiritual pursuits in this life. The spirit, which had a temporary abode in a body and always expressed itself through this medium, is now free to express itself more truly. The spirit is now cast in a new mold where it exists simply as a spirit. It can enjoy supreme bliss for which we had no concept and realization before.

The use of the term *saram khand* has been a matter of some speculation, but it is a term that properly refers to spiritual beauty, effort, or unfoldment. Spiritual beauty, obviously, is not to be confused with physical beauty. It is not beauty that could be compared in relative terms. Each form is unique in its own right. This is an essential stage of our spiritual development because our spirit resides in a human form and, therefore, gets muddied or spoiled by the pressures living a life in a difficult world. It is not ready, as it were, for the greatest experience of all. It needs to be fashioned, or subjected, to a process of unfoldment, so that, in the next stage, the soul is ready to receive divine grace.

Meditation 37

In the realm of divine grace,
You are Supreme and the spirit is pure.
Unless it is desired, nothing else
resides here for sure.

There live warriors, heroes
of great spiritual strength.
Their hearts are immersed in the Divine Name
in all its breadth and length.

And there are celestial goddesses,
maidens, and beauties most divine.
Their graceful looks our words
can hardly define.

They do not die or get deluded
by the limits of their own mental confines.
Their hearts are forever filled
with the sacred love of Divine's.

There live devotees,
who belong to different solar regions.
They are in an eternal bliss,
cherishing the True One's beauteous visions.

In the realm of eternal truth,
lives the formless Supreme Being,
whose glance of one loving grace
is a source of joy and yearning.

There are lands, regions,
and biospheres we are unable to comprehend.
If we start describing them,
we shall never reach the end.

There are myriad worlds upon worlds
in perfect alignment,
all wholly subservient, and acting precisely
as per Your commandment.

What You see brings You happiness,
but what You contemplate,
O Nanak, is as hard as steel
to narrate!

In this meditation, there is a description of the last two realms: the realm of divine grace *(karam khand)* and the realm of eternal truth *(sach khand)*. The realm of divine grace is a very special region where only those who are worthy are admitted. The criteria is not what we have done or achieved but whether or not our devotion has truly moved the divine heart. God bestows or denies grace for reasons that are not for us to speculate. That is why it is customary for people to say grace in the midst of their daily routines.

Who resides in this realm? It is people who are strong in their effort and most advanced in their devotion. These are people who have totally immersed themselves in Ram's name. Ram is a metaphor for the qualities of the Supreme Being; it is the name of the Perfect Being.

The last realm, the realm of eternal truth, is the most central place in the whole universe. It is the source of all divine energy. Although God is everywhere, this is the most sacred of all places because of the extreme concentration of the Higher Spirit. Everything is seen clearly from this hallowed ground. There are continents, worlds, solar systems, and galaxies lined up on all sides for the visual pleasure of the Creator. God mandates precise functions for each of these creations. Divine will is carried out in an instant. God beholds this truly magnificent scene and feels happy. Such are the hidden complexities and intricacies, that to describe this realm is as hard like metal!

Meditation 38

Make self-restraint your oven
and cultivate a master goldsmith's tenderness.
Be informed by an awakened mind
and sharpen the tools of your consciousness.

Let our Beloved's name be the bellows
and atonement be the heat and fire.
In this crucible of love, forge oneness
with the One for whom you aspire.

Fulfillment comes to those
who are blessed with divine grace.
O Nanak, through our Beloved's loving glance,
we attain everlasting blissful grace.

In this last meditation, which is a continuation of the preceding four meditations devoted to the description of the five realms, the Guru presents a design for living that is a blueprint for entry into the higher realms described earlier. We have to learn to be patient. We need to use our understanding as a way of exploring divine knowledge. With the love of God in our heart, we need to find a way of living that conforms to the moral order that is divinely established. Asking for divine grace should become a part of our daily routine. If we are able to win our Beloved's gracious glance, our bliss will be beyond any description.

There are powerful metaphors in this meditation. We have to make continence (self-restraint or moderation) our forge and patience our goldsmith. Let our awakened mind be the anvil and divine knowledge the hammer. God's discipline should be our bellows and an austere way of life should be the heat and fire. Our devotion should be the crucible to melt the sacred word. In such a mint (the little factory of love) the sacred word is coined. These powerful images convey the intensity with which we need to pray in order to gain our entry into higher realms.

Epilogue

Air, the Preceptor; water, the Father;
and earth, the Mother.
Day and night are our nurses,
and we grow in the lap of a foster mother.

Our good and bad actions will be examined
by an impartial judge in true earnestness.
Some of us will be divinely embraced,
while others will fall farther into darkness.

Those who worship the Name
will have their suffering terminated.
O Nanak, with their faces glowing, they
and their loved ones will be emancipated!

The natural order of the universe is the spiritual order. Elements like air, water, and soil are our Beloved's bodily extensions. These life-giving and life-sustaining forces are expressions of divine love for this creation. Without the provision of these ecological necessities, our physical, moral, and spiritual life will be arduous, if not impossible.

Whatever exists in the natural world is meant for the common good. We need to be responsible citizens in how we use these common resources. Our actions determine not only our well-being but also the well-being of generations to come.

God will judge our actions. If we are truthful and moral, and if we have made ourselves worthy of divine love, our labor of living this life time and again will come to an end. Not only shall we benefit ourselves, we may be able to benefit our loved ones. This in essence is the spiritual ladder, a bridge to our Supreme Beloved's home.

Mool Mantra Meditation

Sit in a comfortable position. Do some deep breathing exercises to center your energy. Close your eyes and focus your attention on your forehead or the third eye. Slowly recite the following words of the *Mool* Mantra. This meditation is highly effective and it will open your heart to God's love and compassion. It will strengthen your values and beliefs. It will create feelings of goodwill for other beings. It will deepen your spirituality and devotion. (Recommended time: 30 minutes each morning)

Ikk Oankar	One God
Satnam	True Name
Karta Purakh	Creative Supreme Being
Nirbhau	Without Fear
Nirvair	Loving, Compassionate
Akal Moorat	Immortal Form
Ajooni	Timeless
Saibhang	Self-existent
Gur Prasad	By Grace Obtained

Thirty-nine Most Beautiful Names Mentioned in *Japji* Meditations

Aad	Primal
Ajuni	Immortal
Akal Moorat	Eternal form
Akhri Nam	The Word of God
Anad	Ever-existent
Anahat	Indestructible
Anil	Pure
Ape Ap	Self-existent
Barma	Brahma
Barmao	Brahma
Da-ta	God
Dataar	Benefactor
Devi	Goddess
Gorakh	Vishnu
Gurmukh	Supreme Guru
Ikk	One
Ind	Indra
Isar	Shiva
Jagdis	Deity of the world
Karta	Creator
Nadri	Compassionate, Merciful

Nath	Supreme
Niranjan	Pure, Without blemish
Nirankar	Formless
Nirbhau	Without fear
Nirvair	Without animosity
Oankar	Not changeable, Consistent
Parvati	Parvati (goddess)
Patsah	Ruler
Patsahi Patsah	The Great Sovereign
Purakh	Primal Being, Eternal
Sacha Sahib	Truly empowered
Sachiar	True being
Sachiara	True being
Saibhang	Self-illumined, Self-existent
Sat Nae	True Name
Sat Nam	True Name
Vad-da Daa-ta	Great dispenser of gifts
Vada Sahib	Truly empowered

Part Three

Japji

A Guide to Spiritual Living

Japji
A Guide to Spiritual Living

1. Understanding the True Nature of God

We can establish a spiritually nourishing relationship with God only after we understand what God really *is*. The first thing we need to understand is that God is One. The concept of Oneness of God is common to many spiritual traditions. In the Bible, the Lord declares that "Beside me there is no God," and "There is no God but one." According to the Koran, God is not *a* God but *the* God. In Confucianism, God is equated with absolute truth. In Buddhism, the essential, universal and undifferentiated quality of the Ultimate Reality is called "Suchness," which among other things means Truth (Oneness). In *Vishnu Purana*, a sacred Hindu scripture, Brahma, Vishnu and Shiva are represented as chief energies of Brahman (God), a view similar to that stated by Guru Nanak: all gods and goddesses are manifestations of One True God, who alone is Supreme.

As a source of compassion and grace, God transcends all distinctions of time and place. Some philosophers have looked upon God as a source of what is right and good. There are those who have called God the "eternal mystery," and others claim to have intimate knowledge of the Supreme through simple faith and daily prayer. Many proofs have been offered to show that God exists. These maintain, for example, that if this world is real, with its wondrous landscape, its Creator must also exist. If there is purpose and order in the universe, as we no doubt find at all times, it could not have been possible without a higher force managing it. If we believe that our life has a potential for spiritual experience, there must be a definite source of this goodness.

Guru Nanak equates God with Truth, a view also shared by St. Thomas Aquinas, who wrote that Truth has its source in God. It means that what is true cannot be challenged and it can never be falsified. It describes the everlasting reality, known through faith, not reason. Our experience of true living is a divine experience. It is through this experience that we come closer to the True Name. Guru as a spiritual guide, in this context, is a mediator of Divine Truth.

Truth is a fundamental, divine attribute, and it distinguishes the Supreme Being from all other beings or created objects. It demands perfection which is not possible through the free play of natural forces, or through human birth, which is another step in our quest for perfection. Only the Creator could be above all imperfections, impurities, and falsifications. It is the standard by which everything else is to be measured. When we depart from Truth (as the revealed Word of God), we move away from God.

God is above fear of any kind. Fear is part of our daily life. We are afraid of being harmed; we are afraid that our loved ones will be harmed. More than anything else, we are afraid of being sick, losing our wealth or job, and, above all, of dying. Fear is a recognition that there is a power bigger than us and definitely more brutal than us that can harm us. The harm may be physical or psychological. As long as it lasts, it takes a great emotional toll because it exerts pressure on our nervous system, on our reflexes, and on our ability to think clearly. God is above fear, because nothing exists that is not a part of the divine creation. The source of fear, in order to be credible, has to have a life of its own. What is mortal cannot be a source of worry or concern to one who is immortal.

Also, God is the ultimate source of love and compassion. Love conquers all fear. Compassion destroys all evil, not through any violent reaction, but as a fountain of light that slowly conquers all darkness. Once we get closer to God, we move away from fear. In short, fear is a reflection of our imperfect divinity. Once our life is filled with divine love, fear departs. Where love resides fear has no place. Alternatively, when love disappears, fear takes over. God is without malice, jealousy, or ill will. Love is God's vital attribute—love for all beings, love for all created phenomena. When the Supreme Beloved itself is a fountain of love, feelings of hatred, malice, jealousy, or ill will have no place in the divine realm. But in our own life these things do matter, often creating a field of negative energy around us. When we open ourselves to God, we experience an unstoppable shower of love. We cleanse ourselves of all negativities.

The Bible says, "We love, because He first loved us." In Guru Nanak's spirituality, love is not only an ideal, it is a matter of daily practice. If there is no loving kindness in our hearts, we have no divinity left and we are no different from a beast. In order to practice what we preach, we need to express our love in selfless service to others. The Guru says that without selfless service no lofty objective can be fulfilled; only when we serve selflessly can we earn the merit of pure action.

Love knows no calculation. It does not ask for a return on its "investment." In one of his compositions, Guru

143

Nanak makes the point that a true lover is simply absorbed in love of the Beloved. If the Beloved does not respond, no complaint or frustration is expressed. Such a complaint is frivolous because God's love for us is never in question. If we don't feel it within, we have not looked far enough or deep enough.

In order to receive love, we have to make a gift of love. Giving is actually receiving; we are getting back what we offer, but not many of us look at love this way. Forgiveness is another form of love. Forgiving wrong doing opens our heart to someone who needs love. Sheikh Farid, a Sufi saint whose poetical work is included in *Guru Granth Sahib*, says:

> Those who beat you with fists,
> do not pay them in the same coin.
> Before leaving, kiss their feet.

God, according to Guru Nanak, is formless and thus timeless. Formlessness is not the same thing as emptiness. Formlessness, in reality, is a higher consciousness—a simultaneous awareness of all places and of all beings. God's presence is formless but it is a presence that is felt all the same. We don't see it but we can feel it. According to *Tao Te Ching*, a sacred text of Taoism:

> You look at it, but it is not to be seen
> Its name is Formless.
> You listen to it, but it is not to be heard
> Its name is Soundless.
> You grasp it, but it is not to be held.
> Its name is Bodiless.

This divine attribute of formlessness should remind us of our own formlessness; we are not solid bodies as we appear to be. We are composed of millions of atoms and molecules that move around and evolve within us. Another dimension of our formlessness is our soul that we can't see or touch but which survives our physical body. Our own timelessness is, therefore, a dimension of our formlessness.

2. Leading a Virtuous Life

Guru Nanak divides our spiritual path into five distinct stages: moral living and rightful actions, search for divine knowledge, spiritual unfoldment, divine grace, and the final entry into the realm of Eternal Truth. Each stage is unique and important. These stages appear as part of a sequence and it is not possible for us to by-pass any of these steps. For example, moral living is a precondition for the search of divine knowledge. A person who leads a morally decadent life surely will see no need to search for knowledge of any kind, let alone spiritual knowledge. Also, our spirit cannot unfold unless we have accumulated sufficient spiritual energy during the first two stages. Any further movement from this point onward is possible only when we receive divine grace, which is not our right but a "reward" for good deeds. Leading a virtuous life is the very foundation of our spiritual quest. In order for us to go any farther on the spiritual path, we need to make truthful and moral living an essential part of our life. It is only through such living that we make ourselves worthy of God's compassion and grace.

Growing-up in a world where money can buy more comforts and sensual delights than it was possible at any other time in human history, how can we agree on a set of values and behaviors that would provide a reliable guide to a virtuous life? We need to acknowledge that there are some things which are moral, ethical, doable, and right under any circumstances. We may have a difference of opinion on whether it is moral to charge interest. But there should be no controversy on things like violence, falsehood, exploitation of the poor and helpless. We need to identify some core

145

values around themes which cut across societal and cultural boundaries. These seven core values, based on Guru Nanak's teachings, are:

> *Non-violence.* Avoiding violence that hurts the innocent, kills, insults (in the form of rape or other degrading actions) the victim; mass killings of innocent people in a war or a political conflict.

> *Truth.* Letting the reality appear in its pure form. Separating facts from opinions. Not using falsehood of any kind to deceive other people. Treating truthful living as a sacred obligation.

> *Love.* Showing sympathy and compassion for a victim of oppression, having a sense of justice, keeping a charitable spirit, sharing one's wealth and good fortune with the poor and needy.

> *Virtue.* Pursuit of highest personal morality in one's daily life, respecting the honor and integrity of one's partner, taking responsibility for one's children, catering to their material, emotional and intellectual needs, caring for the needs of elders in the family.

> *Communitarianism.* Being a good citizen, participating in electoral processes, raising voice against misdeeds of those in authority; using public office for public good; protecting natural environment; giving one's employer a fair share of one's time, talent and ability.

> *Equality.* Treating all people as equal despite differences of color, race, gender, or ethnic origins; respecting cultural and spiritual traditions of other people.

> *Theism.* Having faith in the unbounded love, mercy and compassion of the Creator for all things and all beings.

This is not an attempt to define a new morality. It has not been easy for moral philosophers who have struggled with these issues over the ages. We can look at various shades of opinions, or what our own belief system has to say about these matters, but, in the end, we need to have an objective look at how we are coping with difficult moral and ethical choices in our life. This freedom for self-evaluation is not a blank check, meaning whatever serves our needs or purposes is acceptable. What it means is that we need to cultivate, in the words of Albert Einstein, a "moral attitude in and toward life" based on the totality of our being—body, mind and soul. Not to do this self-evaluation in a serious way would indicate our reluctance to follow a spiritual path.

3. Caring for Others and Showing Compassion

The Guru celebrates the unity of people who love and worship God. The lovers of God are encouraged to spend time together in religious activities, in recitation of the Name, in sharing their blessings and sorrows, and (although it might look simple) eating food together. This sense of belonging and spiritual bonding is the nourishment they need to expand their reach into the unknown. Therefore, we have to be caring and compassionate human beings.

Guru Arjun Dev, the fifth guru, explains the reason for all believers to have a sense of belonging. We are residents, he says, of the city founded by God. The Founder is the source of all blessings and joys. It is only in being together that our objectives are fulfilled. When people are together, they do not cause pain or injury to one another. When peace comes to a small number of people, it gradually extends to all of humankind. And in peace and contemplation lies the path of self-realization.

4. Realizing that Actions Have Consequences

We may be condemned to repeat our journey or even regress, in terms of our spiritual development. This is the lesson of karma or predestination. As we sow, so shall we eat, says Guru Nanak. This idea, known as the Golden Rule, appears in every major wisdom tradition in one form or another:

> The true role of life is to guard and do by the things of others as they do on their own. (Hinduism)

Whatever is hurtful to yourself, do not to your fellowman. This is the whole of the law, the rest is merely commentary. (Judaism)
Hurt not others in ways that you yourself would find hurtful. (Buddhism)
Regard your neighbor's gain as your own gain and your neighbor's loss as your own loss. (Taoism)
Do not unto others what you would not have them do unto you. (Confucianism)
As you give, so shall you receive. (Christianity)
No one of you is a believer until he desires for his brother that which he desires for himself. (Islam)

But what happens when we don't live by these, or other, golden rules? We end up having karmic accumulation, that is undesirable for the evolution of our soul. There is a way, says Guru Nanak, to combat this karmic cycle. Prayer, worship, meditation, moral living: all these modes of spiritual life will help us gain divine grace, which means that with our own effort we can reverse negative karmic energy into something positive. But if we continue to hurt other people, and spend our entire life in material attachments, we can't hope to gain enlightenment. The forceful cycle of karma will continue to exact its toll.

God is omnipresent and omniscient. We cannot hide anything from the all-seeing Eye of God. It watches all our actions. There is a precise measurement, in the sense that the standard applied is fair, objective, and compassionate. In a way, this is the logical extension of the Law of Karma. Although this accounting is perfect, what we get in practice is determined by several factors, the most important of which is divine grace. We have to accept whatever comes our way. As Guru Nanak says:

> Nanak, for human beings, it is idle to ask for pleasure
> when suffering comes;
> pleasure and suffering are robes that we must wear.
> Where arguing is of no avail, it is best to be contented.

Var Majh

148

Also:

> After we leave this world,
> we are asked to give an account of our deeds,
> which are already recorded in the divine register.
> We can't escape or rebel against this.
> We are caught in a blind alley and there is no place to go.
> Says Nanak, destroy the falsehood
> and let the truth prevail.

Ramkali-ki-Var

5. Becoming Socially Responsive and a Catalyst for Positive Change

Our society, culture, and economic system are all part of the bigger order created for us by God. But at the microlevel, subsystems are humanly designed and implemented and, thus, are imperfect and unjust in several ways. Only divine order is perfect and just. If we accept and submit ourselves to divine order, we can bring perfection to our social and economic institutions. It is, therefore, important to acknowledge that "in God we trust" is an initial required affirmation to make in order to live in the kingdom of God and to establish supremacy of an order based on superordinate values. A society that does not trust in God manifests itself as a tyranny and, thus, disintegrates under the weight of its own contradictions.

Guru Nanak advocates rule of law and exercise of power by the common will of the people. He says:

> The ruler who submits to democratic ideals,
> his rule is lasting.

Maru

Therefore, democracy is not only a human innovation; it is a reflection of the will of God, something borrowed by us from

149

the divine order that the Creator had in mind for us. In view of this, all dictatorial regimes are violations of divine order. They crush the human spirit, making the journey of the soul more hazardous and tortuous. A free society, where people have a voice and freedom to practice their religion and spiritual values, is heaven on earth. Corrupt and oppressive regimes are reflective of hell and are a domain of Satan.

As we relinquish ourselves to the loving care of God, we release spiritual energy that has the capacity to work for us and to promote the common good. This energy has a great "healing touch," not only for individual ailments but for social pathologies, such as crime, poverty, and social alienation. Spiritual life, in practice, is a life devoted to the well-being of community. Spiritual life and communal life, therefore, go hand in hand.

God-centered people, according to Guru Nanak, are not self-centered. They think of themselves as a small part of the much bigger social organism. This harmony between the individual and the community occurs spontaneously, without any personal effort. Selfishly living for ourselves is a very narrow attitude in view of all the possibilities that life has to offer. Once we become role models for others, we start to radiate our spiritual energy to benefit those around us. That is why *Japji* says that devotees, men and women who truly believe in God, not only immortalize themselves but also help their loved ones—friends, family members, and associates—to manage the difficult transition from the material to the spiritual life, and even beyond to an immortal life.

A spiritual life lived in accordance with divine order can have a great effect on our inner and outer existence. There is no real separation between body and soul. We need to take care of our physical body to provide a suitable environment for our soul to gain its own unfoldment. Guru Nanak attaches great importance to personal cleanliness, proper nourishment, outdoor activities, and community service.

6. Leading Our Life in Accordance With Our Personal Sense of Right and Wrong.

We need to nurture and develop our own personal ethic to guide our values and behaviors. This personal ethic may be drawn from our religious convictions, or our moral temperament that we owe to our parents or spiritual mentors. It is not a one-time effort. It is the job of a lifetime. We need to reinforce our personal values through the use of appropriate myths, metaphors, rituals or whatever other avenues for spiritual development are available to us.

Religious orthodoxy in India takes the view that the evil we do in this life can be cleansed by a variety of ritualistic actions. Guru Nanak is opposed to such actions as they do not add any spiritual value. It is only through total inner transformation and not through the performance of outward actions that we realize God.

Whether rituals are good or bad is not an easy question to settle. Possibly, there are beneficial rituals that can add richness and variety to our spiritual life. But we have to be careful how we define the term. If "ritual" is performing an action with one's free will, with the conscious understanding that it would add worth to one's life, then there is no harm done in performing that action. For example, all actions performed by choice, such as participating in a religious activity, contributing to a charity, reading from a particular scripture at an appointed hour, visiting holy places in the spirit of discovery, or enchantments of daily life such as taking a walk, writing a journal, playing a musical instrument are all healthy and they provide nourishment for our soul, in addition to enhancing our commitment to a values driven life. The critical test is whether rituals are facilitating our inner transformation, or are these symbols of an outward life, without any direct connection with our "soul work."

7. Understanding that We Are Spiritually Evolving Beings

This universe is an extraordinary creation of God. It is boundless in material possessions and boundaryless in terms of its geographic expanse. There is no visible end to the planets, solar systems and galaxies. Even the best of science can't keep track of the number because, with every scientific advance, new discoveries of galaxies are made. The secret of creation is the biggest mystery of all, which is known only to its Creator. We should respect this mystery and refrain from making unfounded claims.

How was this universe created? There are creation myths in many cultures that say that God, or a power subordinate to God, created this universe, which emerged only in response to the fulfillment of the wishes of the Creator. Another view (which is considered a scientific view) holds that this world is the result of a long evolutionary process, spread over five billion years. Human beings, animals, and plants, have evolved over time from primitive chemical substances through processes of diversification and modification. Although human offspring inherit a resemblance to their parents, they are not identical. Evolution, according to the Darwinian interpretation, proceeds by natural selection of well-adapted individuals over a span of several centuries. It is primarily driven by mutation changes. According to the most recent research, species tend to remain stable over long periods of time and then to change abruptly. On the face of it, these two views are incompatible. Many people see a conflict here. The world could not be a creation of God and also an object that is evolving on its own. To a logical mind, this does not appear convincing.

However, in reality, creation and evolution are not either-or propositions.

Creation is a religious or spiritual idea. Evolution is a human discovery. Guru Nanak resolves the conflict between these positions. This universe is an act of creation, that is, a creation by a loving and caring God. But this creation is also the starting point of an evolutionary process that has gone on for millions of years, an evolution that unfolds the will of God in ways that are difficult for us to comprehend.

In the following composition, Guru Nanak develops the theme of transition from physical creation to spiritual evolution. The physical world was created and left to evolve from the interplay of natural forces. But the human world, with the human body at its center, was created with divine consciousness lodged at the pinnacle of human consciousness. Therefore, as human beings evolve spiritually, reaching upward to the highest levels of consciousness, they evolve from the lowest level of physical creation to the highest level of super consciousness. That is how a simple being becomes an enlightened being. The underlying process is nothing except the spiritual evolution.

> For countless years, there was nothing except darkness;
> there was no earth, no heaven, only the Will of God.
> There was no day or night, no sun or moon;
> and the Creator was absorbed in a deep meditation.
>
> There was no creation, no sound, no wind, no water.
> There was no being or non-being or transition from one
> to the other.
> There were no regions, no seas, no rivers or flowing waters.
>
> There was no heaven, mortal world, or lower region;
> neither hell nor heaven nor time that perished the living.
> Concepts of hell and heaven, birth and death, were yet unknown.

There were no Brahma, Vishnu, or Shiva;
Only One Sole Presence was felt.
There were no male or female, caste, or birth.
There was no suffering, no joy.

There was no saint, no benevolent soul, no forest dweller;
There were no fully formed, toiling, or lazy beings.
There was no yogi, no fully realized person.

There was no meditation, no austerity.
And no one talked of not this, not this [duality].
The Supreme created and valued Itself.

There was no initiation, no rosary for prayer.
There were no gopis, no Krishna, no cows or cowboys.
There was no magic, no spells, trickery, or soothing music.

There were no preferred actions, religions, or wealth attachments.
No one noticed one's caste at birth.
There were no attachments, no fears of death, no need to meditate.

There was no shame, no soul, no life.
There were no saints, no godlings.
There was no divine knowledge, no account of creation.

There was no higher or lower caste.
The was no god, no temple, no invocation.
There were no offerings, no fasts, no worships.

There was no scholar or judge.
There was no preacher, no one atoning, no pilgrimage.
There was no ruler, no subject, no high-sounding name.

There was no love, no devotion, no mind, no matter.
There was no friend or blood relation.
The Supreme, at Its pleasure, became a banker or a merchant.

There were no denominational books to read.
No prayers for sunrise or sunset.
The Supreme was the speaker who saw everything.

At Its pleasure, the world was created.
And without any support, the creation was sustained.
Brahma, Vishnu, and Shiva were created, and the love of the
material world.

To a chosen few, God gave the Word.
The Supreme watched Its creation with loving care.
Within continents, solar systems, and lower regions,
the Supreme manifested Itself.

The Creator remained unattached but carved the human body
as the most sacred center of the universe.
The body was created combining elements of air, water and fire.

The Creator created the nine zones of human consciousness;
and in the tenth zone divine energy was lodged—unknowable
and limitless.
Seven seas of immaculate water were created to wash away dirt.

The lamps of sun and the moon were created to reflect
divine light.
By creating them the Supreme celebrated Its' own glory.
The Supreme became the source of honor and glory.

When blessings were received, death held no fear.
The devotee stood like a lotus flower in the water and remembered.

With the Supreme's command, the sky is opened.
With the Supreme's blessings, life abounds under, over, and above
the earth.
With the Supreme's blessings, we breathe and sustain ourselves.

Maru Sohale

As Guru Nanak's composition reveals, evolution occurs at two
levels: the physical level, which is easily measurable, and the
spiritual level, which is basically unseen. Spiritual evolution
symbolizes the advancement of our individual and collective
consciousness.

8. Making Nature Our Spiritual Guide and Companion

Nature is the most beautiful part of our planet. We assume that in other worlds there are natural systems that may be even more beautiful. Nature is clearly the imagination and the work of a Supreme Artist. There is, therefore, something sacred about nature that must be acknowledged. Nature, without doubt, is a vehicle for our spiritual advancement.

If the connection between nature and God is true, it follows that nature has sanctity far beyond the economic rationale of being simply a "natural resource" that is available to us for our comfort and profit. We should become custodians of this resource instead of being silent spectators of its ruthless exploitation and destruction. We should truly make it our spiritual guide and companion.

We once asked a group of nature lovers as to why they thought nature was sacred. We were surprised to find specific examples of why these people had made nature a part of their spiritual quest. Some typical responses:

> Nature is the cradle of great cultural and spiritual traditions, most prominently American Indian but also indigenous peoples around the world.

> Nature is our accompaniment in the process of gaining enlightenment. Buddha got enlightenment under a tree. Himalayas were traditionally the home of Rishis in the ancient Vedic period. God spoke to Moses from inside the burning bush.

> Forest in Eastern and Western mythologies is a place of wonder and amusement. As Joseph Campbell used to say, the hero, in his search for spiritual fulfillment, never enters the forest where there is a well-trodden path. Like the spirit, forest hides what it has in store for us. However, it never disappoints.

Many religious scriptures, including the Bible and the Koran, describe in vivid detail our connection with the earth, air, sky and water.

The changing colors of nature, including change of seasons, represent our changing moods, periods of our moral and spiritual growth, and the uniqueness of our personalities.

Nature is our connection with the rest of the universe. When we look at the forest, we can see the sky beyond it, we can see the stars, galaxies, and the whole dance of the universe.

Nature has a spiritual and cultural dimension, but also it is a practical asset for the preservation of human race based on many useful functions performed by it. Recently, *New York Times**carried a story which stated that scientists have now succeeded in assigning a dollar value to the essential services performed by the natural world. The most interesting part of the story actually was the description of seventeen categories of services provided by nature that *Times* reproduced from the *Nature* magazine. These categories included:

Gas regulation: Carbon dioxide/oxygen balance, ozone ultraviolet protection.
Climate regulation: Greenhouse gas regulation.
Disturbance regulation: Storm protection, flood control, drought recovery.
Water regulation: Provision of water for irrigation, mills or transportation.
Water supply: Provision of water for irrigation, reservoirs and aquifers.
Erosion control and sediment retention: prevention of soil loss by wind, runoff, etc.; storage of silt in lakes and wetlands.
Soil formation: Weathering of rock and accumulation of organic material.
Nutrient cycling: nitrogen fixation.
Waste treatment: Pollution control, detoxification.
Pollination: Pollination for plant reproduction.
Biological control: Predator control of prey species.

* *New York Times*, C5, May 20, 1997

Refuges: Nurseries, habitat for migratory species.
Food production: Production of fish, game, crops, nuts and fruits by hunting, fishing, gathering or subsistence farming.
Raw materials: Production of lumber, fuel or fodder.
Genetic resources: Medicines, resistance genes for crops, ornamental plant species, pets.
Recreation: Ecotourism, sports, fishing, other outdoor recreation.
Cultural: Esthetic, artistic, educational, spiritual and scientific values of ecosystems.

If nature is so critical for our survival as human species, how can we strengthen our bonds with it? There are many practical suggestions from the literature in what has come to be known as "deep ecology." Here are few practical things we can do:

Understand the way nature works.
Understand the natural harmony that exists between individuals, communities, and nature.
Simplify wants; cut down on the consumption of non-essentials.
Aim to meet only the vital needs and recycle.
Help create decentralized, nonhierarchical, and democratic systems and structures.
Recognize that nature has intrinsic worth.
Remember that a species extinct once is gone forever.
Remember that when we destroy nature, we destroy ourselves.

9. Never, Ever, Forgetting God

Sinful conduct can manifest itself in several ways. The greatest sin of all is to forget God, to forget that we live in a world that God made for us. The denial of our own divinity is, therefore, the biggest sin. Who are the people who forget God? They are generally those who are so consumed by their success in life that they forget their own Creator. Little do they realize that there are many ups and downs in our life. We do remember God in times of need. But if we are true to ourselves, if we are aware of the mystery that surrounds us in the form of this universe about which we have no clue, if we are conscious of our own mortality, we will never forget the Supreme Being who gave us the most precious gift of all—the breath of life.

The Koran says: "… remembrance of God is the greatest thing in life, without doubt." We once posed the following question to a group of people: Why do you think it is important to remember God? Here are some of the answers they gave us:

> God answers my prayers, but many times I do not even realize that my prayer has been answered.

> When I talk to God, people think I'm a religious person, but when God talks to me, people think I have gone crazy.

> I always pass on my worries and concerns to God and feel light as a feather.

> God keeps my door to the lounge of temptation permanently locked.

> The very thought of God washes my soul of its sins.

> God is the sailing ship that carries us through the stormy seas of this life to the floating white clouds of the next one.

> If I forgot God, I will cease to be a moral being.

> I can't forget God because I never stop seeing beauty and goodness in this world. Who else is behind all this?

> God is an answer as well as a question. The answer requires contemplation. The question is the eternal mystery.

10. Monitoring Our Spiritual Progress

The length of time lived, measured in months and years, is not as important as the quality of life itself, particularly the spiritual content. Do we spend our life doing good? Do we remember God? Do we spend time in meditation? Our faith (higher moral values and commitments and a strong belief system) can play an important role in keeping us strong to fight repression and injustice, helping us withstand various temptations, and even making sacrifices for worthy causes.

When we decide to lead a spiritual life, it causes us to look differently at our priorities. How do we spend our time? What are the things that are most important to us? It is, therefore, important to keep track of our spiritual progress. Guru Nanak asks us to pay attention to our preferred way of life:

> Our nights are spent sleeping,
> our days in pursuit of physical needs.
> This life, which is as precious as a jewel
> goes for a sea-shell.
> What an act of foolishness!
> If we don't spend our time in God realization,
> we will regret a lot in the end.

Gauri Bairagini

Also:

> Realization of Truth is higher than all else;
> higher still is truthful living.

Sri Raga Ashtpadi

11. Making Poetry and Music a Tool for Enlightenment

Poetry and music are important in many sacred traditions; they are more so in the spiritual tradition established by Guru Nanak. Although *Japji* is not supposed to be sung (it is meant to be read slowly), other compositions of Guru Nanak were written for specific ragas in the Indian classical tradition. All compositions in *Guru Granth Sahib* are in verse, and they are

160

supposed to be sung in the prescribed ragas. The Guru's fondness for music is evident in several passages. Music is a divine craft suitable for gods and goddesses and poetry is the medium through which the soul expresses itself.

Spiritual philosopher, Thomas Moore, writes in his book, *The Re-Enchantment of Everyday Life* : " We know ... from countless paintings of angels that there is a music that is truly heavenly, not of this world. Or could it be that music and soul-stirring sounds link our daily life to eternal things? Ficino said that music comes to us on air that has been tempered by sound, sets in motion the air spirit of the person, and then effects the heart and penetrates to the most intimate levels of the mind. And this music is directly tied to the music of the world, its rhythms and modalities." (p. 111)

12. Conquering Our Ego-Mind

What is ego? Swami Ramakrishna once used an analogy to clarify the distinction between ego and soul. Think of an old-style horse carriage, he said. The person sitting above the horses and driving the carriage is our ego-mind. The person who is inside the carriage is our soul—the real owner. As long as ego is doing the driving, we go here and there, without any sense of direction, trying to control everything that comes our way. But when our soul is awakened and it takes charge, we find our true destination.

People with strong ego have an inflated view of their physical and mental capacities, they love to demean other people and their potential, and they display all kind of bad behaviors in their interactions with others. Conquering the ego-mind is, therefore, the biggest battle for all human beings. Once we are able to subdue our controlling tendencies, we start to look upon life in a different way. Flow comes back into our life. We open our mind to new ideas, new possibilities. The door to our personal transformation is opened and we become more loving, more compassionate, and more sensitive. But this door to self-transformation can be opened only with strong self-determination.

Our ego-mind also breeds ignorance, creating wrong notions about ourselves and the world. We are unable to face reality. We start to filter information. Such an attitude slows our mental and spiritual advancement. Ignorance, nourished by the ego-mind, can take many forms: we may be ignorant of our purpose in life and our relationship with God, or we commit acts of violence or injustice against others who are helpless to defend themselves. People who rob, rape, terrorize, mutilate or injure other people are ignorant of the consequences of their actions. Once we start nourishing our soul, and, in return, our soul starts nourishing us, our ego slowly withers away, making our life fruitful for us, our family members, and our friends.

13. Experiencing Mental Balance, Tranquillity and Contentment

Mental balance, tranquillity, and contentment are very important in a world full of choices and opportunities. If our contentment depends on the level of our material acquisitions, we would never reach a point where we would be fully satisfied. On the other hand, if we adopt contentment as a way of life, it would be unaffected by our daily gains and losses. We will have happiness in all periods of our life.

Honest effort is the only real effort that counts. With honest effort we can move ahead, we can achieve our life goals, and we can be truly proud of our attainments. But some of us think that there are short cuts, that we can move ahead quicker if we compromise our principles and our integrity, that what counts is the result and not the means. This is faulty logic. There

is no choice between means and ends. We need right out-
comes using right means.

Self-restraint complements mental contentment and
honest effort. People who can restrain their desires and im-
pulses are more likely to be honest in their efforts and have
greater peace of mind. The many choices and temptations
that are offered by the consumer society in which we live
make self-restraint a necessity. We need to center our mind.
Says Guru Nanak:

> The restless mind is not centered at one place;
> like a deer, it nibbles at tender shoots.
> If we were to lodge in our mind the divine lotus feet,
> we will live longer with an awakened mind.
> All human beings suffer from anxiety,
> but by contemplation of God comes bliss.
>
> *Ramkali Dakhni Onkar*

When we are fully contented, we are touched by a
presence that is much larger than our own life. The sacred
touch, by necessity, is a tender touch. Tenderness and sensi-
tivity thus become essential dimensions of our humanity.
There can be no love without caring for others' feelings.
People who are rude or disrespectful in their behavior, who
are insensitive to human suffering, have only one thing in
common: they have shut love out of their lives to pursue
other objectives. They seem to forget that when love goes
out of their lives, nothing much is left.

We have a hidden treasure, Guru Nanak reminds us,
inside all of us. However, most of the time we are unaware
of what we are capable of achieving. Self-discovery of our
true potential is not possible without getting in touch with
our inner core. This is the function of meditation. It is only
in true silence, when all internal dialogue is suspended, that

we start to discover who we really are. It is through the process of finding our own divinity that we discover ourselves.

14. Praying for Divine Grace

Divine grace is the central pillar of Guru Nanak's spirituality. Thus, it finds a prominent place in several meditations of *Japji*. If the Creator is not pleased, nothing will ever be gained. Divine grace is an essential condition we must fulfill to reach our ultimate goal in life. Personal transformation is possible at all times. Sinners can turn into pious beings if they take the path of virtue, conquer their ego-mind, and ask for divine forgiveness. It is never too late. This goal is always within our reach. Says Guru Nanak:

> Always in love with created beings,
> Creator is a custodian of our well-being.
> O Savior, invaluable are Your blessings;
> without any limit is Your power to bestow merit.
>
> *Kirtan Sohila*

Human effort alone is not enough. There is a stage in our spiritual evolution where we do not progress any farther without the gift of divine grace. Only when we are divinely blessed can we climb all the five steps on the spiritual ladder and finally reach the Mansion of our Supreme Beloved.

SUMMING-UP
A Guide to Spiritual Living

1. Understanding the True Nature of God
2. Leading a Virtuous Life
3. Caring for Others and Showing Compassion
4. Realizing that Actions Have Consequences
5. Becoming Socially Responsible and a Catalyst for Positive Change
6. Leading Our Life in Accordance With Our Personal Sense of Right and Wrong
7. Understanding that We Are Spiritually Evolving Beings
8. Making Nature Our Spiritual Guide and Companion
9. Never, Ever, Forgetting God
10. Monitoring Our Spiritual Progress
11. Making Poetry and Music a Tool for Enlightenment
12. Conquering Our Ego-Mind
13. Experiencing Mental Balance, Tranquillity and Contentment
14. Praying for Divine Grace

Bibliography

Anthony, Carol K. *A Guide to the I Ching.* Stow, MA: Anthony Publishing Company, 1988.

Armstrong, Karen. *A History of God.* New York: Alfred A. Knopf, 1993.

Barrett, Richard. *Spiritual Unfoldment: A Guide to Liberating Your Soul.* Alexandria, VA: Unfoldment Publications, 1995.

Barks, Coleman with John Moyne. *The Essential Rumi.* New York: HarperSanFrancisco, 1995.

Belitz, Charlene and Meg Lundstrom. *The Power of Flow.* New York: Harmony Books, 1997.

Blau, Evelyne. *Krishnamurti 100 Years.* New York: Stewart, Tabori & Chang, 1995.

Bly, Robert. *Iron John: A Book About Men.* New York: Addison-Wesley, 1990.

Branden, Nathaniel. *The Art of Living Consciously.* New York: Simon Schuster, 1997.

Brussat, Frederic and Mary Ann. *Spiritual Literacy: Reading the Sacred in Everyday Life.* New York: Scribner, 1996.

Campbell, Joseph. *The Hero With a Thousand Faces.* Princeton, NJ: Princeton University Press, 1949.

Chittister, Joan. *There Is a Season*. Maryknoll, NY: Orbis Books, 1995.

Chopra, Deepak. *Ageless Body, Timeless Mind: The Quantum Alternative to Growing Old*. New York: Harmony Books, 1993.

_____. *Creating Affluence*. San Rafael, CA: New World Library, 1993.

_____. *The Seven Spiritual Laws of Success*. San Rafael, CA: Amber-Allen Publishing, 1994.

_____. *The Way of the Wizard*. New York: Harmony Books, 1995.

Cole, W. Owen. *The Guru in Sikhism*. London: Darton, Longman & Todd, 1982.

_____. *Sikhism and its Indian Context 1469-1708*. London: Darton, Longman and Todd, 1984.

_____. *Sikhism*. Lincolnwood, IL. : N.T.C. Publishing Group, 1994.

Dawood, N.J., tr. *The Koran*. Harmondworth, Middlesex: Penguin Books, 1956.

Duggal, K.S. *Sikh Gurus: Their Lives and Teachings*. Honesdale, PA.: The Himalayan International Institute of Yoga Science and Philosophy of the U.S.A., 1987.

Dreher, Diane. *The Tao of Inner Peace*. New York: HarperPerennial, 1990.

Dyer, Wayne R. *Manifest Your Destiny*. New York: HarperCollins Publishers, 1997.

Estes, Clarissa Pinkola. *Women Who Run With the Wolves*. New York: Balantine Books, 1992.

Fadiman, James and Robert Frager, eds. *Essential Sufism*. New York: HarperSanFrancisco, 1997.

Feinstein, David and Stanley Krippner. *The Mythic Path*. New York: A Jeremy P. Tarcher/Putnam Books, 1997.

Feng, Gia-Fu and Jane English, tr. *Tao Te Ching*. New York: Vintage Books, 1972.

Foundation For Inner Peace. *A Couse In Miracles*. Glen Ellen, CA., 1975.

Fox, Everett. *The Five Books of Moses*. New York: Schocken Books, 1995.

Gawain, Shakti. *Creative Visualization*. New York: Bantam Books, 1978.

Gersten, Dennis. *Are You Getting Enlightened Or Losing Your Mind?* New York: Harmony Books, 1997.

Gibran, Kahlil. *The Prophet*. New York: Alfred A. Knopf., 1988.

Goleman, Daniel. *The Meditative Mind: The Varieties of Meditative Experience*. New York: Jeremy P. Tarcher/Perigee Books, 1988.

Goldstein, Joseph. *Insight Meditation: The Practice of Freedom*. Boston, MA: Shambhala, 1993.

Han, Thich Nhat. *The Miracle of Mindfulness*. Boston, MA: Beacon Press, 1975.

_____. *Peace Is Every Step: The Path of Mindfulness*. New York: Bantam Books, 1991.

_____. *The Blooming of a Lotus*. Boston, MA: Beacon Press, 1993.

Harvey, Andrew. *The Way of Passion*. Berkeley, CA: Frog, Ltd., 1994.

_____, ed. *The Essential Mystics: The Soul's Journey into Truth*. New York: HarperSanFrancisco, 1996..

_____. *Light Upon Light: Inspirations from Rumi*. Berkeley, CA: North Atlantic Books, 1996.

Hawley, John Stratton, and Mark Juergensmeyer. *Songs of the Saints of India*. New York: Oxford University Press, 1988.

Holy Bible, The. (King James Version). n.d. Cleveland: The World Publishing Company.

Judith, Anodea. *Eastern Body Western Mind: Psychology and the Chakra System as a Path to the Self*. Berkeley, CA: Celestial Arts, 1996.

Jacobi, Jolande and R.F.C. Hull, eds. *C.G. Jung Psychological Reflections: A New Anthology of His Writings 1905-1961*. Princeton, NJ: Princeton University Press, 1953.

Kabat-Zinn, Jon. *Full Catastrophe Living: Using the Wisdom of Your Body and Mind to Face Stress, Pain, and Illness*. New York: Delta Books, 1990.

_____. *Wherever You Go There You Are*. New York: Hyperion, 1994.

Kazantzakis, Nikos. *The Saviors of God: Spiritual Exercises*. New York: Simon Schuster, 1969.

Khan, Hazrat Inayat. *The Complete Sayings*. New Lebanon: Omega Publications, Inc., 1978.

Kornfield, Jack. *A Path With Heart*. New York: Bantam Books, 1993.

_____ and Christina Feldman. *Soul Food*. New York: HarperSanFrancisco, 1996.

Krishnamurti, J. *The Book of Life*. New York: HarperSanFrancisco, 1995.

Ladinsky, Daniel. *I Heard God Laughing: Renderings of Hafiz*. Walnut Creek, CA: Sufism Reoriented, 1996.

Lobell, John. *Joseph Campbell: The Man & His Ideas*. New York: Joseph Campbell Foundation, 1993.

Macauliffe, Max Arthur. *The Sikh Religion*. Vols. 1 & 2. Delhi: Low Price Publications, 1990.

McLeod, W.H. *Guru Nanak and the Sikh Religion*. Oxford: Clarendon Press, 1968.

_____. *Textual Sources for the Study of Sikhism*. Chicago: The University of Chicago Press, 1984.

Moore, Thomas. *Care of the Soul*. New York: HaperCollins Publishers, 1992.

_____. *Soul Mates: Honoring the Mysteries of Love and Relationship*. New York: HarperCollins Publishers, 1994.

_____. *The Re-Enchantment of Everyday Life*. New York: HarperCollins Publishers, 1996.

Moyers, Bill. *Genesis: A Living Conversation*. New York: Doubleday, 1997.

Novak, Philip. *The World's Wisdom: Sacred Texts of World's Religions*. New York: HarperSanFrancisco, 1994.

Osbon, Diane K. *Reflections on the Art of Living: A Joseph Campbell Companion*. New York: HarperCollins Publishers, 1991.

Radhakrishnan, S. and Charles E. Moore, eds. *A Sourcebook in Indian Philosophy*. Princeton, NJ: Princeton University Press, 1957.

Radhakrishnan, S. *The Bhagvadgita*. New Delhi: INDUS, 1993.

_____. *The Principal Upanisads*. New Delhi: INDUS, 1994.

Rinpoche, Sogyal. *The Tibetan Book of Living and Dying*. New York: HarperSanFrancisco, 1992.

Satir, Virginia. *Meditations & Inspirations*. Berkeley, CA: Celestial Arts, 1985.

Simpkinson, Charles and Anne Simpskin, eds. *Sacred Stories*. New York: HarperSanFrancisco, 1993.

Singh, Khushwant. *Hymns of Guru Nanak*. New Delhi: Orient Longman, 1969.

Smith, Huston. *The Illustrated World's Religions: A Guide to Our Wisdom Traditions*. New York: HarperSanFrancisco, 1994.

Statton, Elizabeth K. *Seeds of Light*. New York: Simon Schuster, 1997.

Suzuki, Shunryu. *Zen Mind, Beginner's Mind*. New York: Weatherhill, 1970.

Talib, Gurbachan Singh. trans. *Sri Guru Granth Sahib*. 4 vols. Patiala: Punjabi University, 1984 -.

Templeton, John Marks. *Worldwide Laws of Life*. Philadelphia, PA: Templeton Foundation Press, 1997.

Tomlinson, Gerald. *Treasury of Religious Quotations*. Englewood Cliffs, N.J.: Prentice Hall, 1991.

Vardey, Lucinda, ed. *God In All Worlds: An Anthology of Contemporary Spiritual Writing*. New York: Pantheon Books, 1995.

Walsch, Neale Donald. *Conversations with God*. book 1. New York: G.P. Putnam's Sons, 1996.

Ward, Tim. *The Great Dragon's Fleas*. Berkeley, CA: Celestial Arts, 1993.

_____. *What The Buddha Never Taught*. Toronto: Somerville House Publishing, 1993.

_____. *Arousing the Goddess*. Toronto: Somerville House Publishing, 1996.

White, John. *What Is Enlightenment?* New York: Paragon House, 1995.

Whyte, David. *The Heart Aroused*. New York: Currency Doubleday, 1994.

Williamson, Marianne. *A Return to Love*. New York: HarperPerennial, 1992.

Wilson, Andrew, ed. *World Scripture: A Comparative Anthology of Sacred Texts.* New York: Paragon House, 1995.

Yogananda, Paramahansa. *Wine of the Mystic: The Rubaiyat of Omar Khayyam* (A *Spiritual Interpretation*). Los Angeles, CA: Self-Realization Fellowship, 1994.

_____. *The Bhagavad Gita.* 2 vol. Los Angeles, CA: Self-Realizaion Fellowship, 1996.

Zukav, Gary. *The Seat of the Soul.* New York: Simon and Schuster, 1989.

About the Authors

Surinder Deol is the coauthor of *Managing Intercultural Negotiations* and author/editor of two other books on development banking. He works as a senior learning specialist in an international development bank based in Washington, D.C. Mrs. Daler Deol has taught political science at the University of Delhi and has published three books on political theory, *Marxism and Liberalism, Comparative Government & Politics,* and *Charisma and Commitment.* They are available for workshop and public speaking engagements.

Permissions

Grateful acknowledgment is made for permission to reprint the following materials: Selected excerpts reproduced on pages 15-16 from *Textual Sources for the Study of Sikhism,* edited and translated by W.H. McLeod. Copyright © 1984 by W. H. McLeod. Reprinted by permission of Chicago University Press. Selected excerpts reproduced on pages 12, 21, 24, 148-49, 160, 163-64 from *Sri Guru Granth Sahib,* translation by Gurbachan Singh Talib. Copyright © 1984 by Gurbachan Singh Talib. Reprinted by permission of Punjabi University, Patiala, India. Selected excerpts reproduced on pages 153-55 from *Sri Guru Granth Sahib,* translation by Manmohan Singh. Copyright © 1965, 1982, 1991 by Shiromini Gurudwara Prabandhak Committee (SGPC). Reprinted by permission of SGPC. Six lines reproduced on page 144 from *Lao Tzu: Tao Te Ching* by D.C. Lau (editor and translator). Copyright © 1963 by D.C. Lau. Reprinted by permission of Penguin Books, London. Seven lines reproduced on page 161 from *The Re-Enchantment of Everyday Life* by Thomas Moore. Copyright © by Thomas Moore. Reprinted by permission of HarperCollins Publishers.

ORDER FORM

Order a copy of *Japji: The Path of Devotional Meditation*

Give a Gift of Love, a Gift of Japji

Mail to:

_____

_____

_____

_____

Add a Message:

_____

_____

_____

_____

_____

Send a check for US$ 18.00 (including shipping and handling) to:

Mount Meru Books
P. O. Box 27502
Washington, D. C. 20038-7502